GRAY
MATTER

Brain Development

GRAY
MATTER

GRAY
MATTER

Brain Development

Lakshmi Bangalore, Ph.D.

Series Editor
Eric H. Chudler, Ph.D.

CHELSEA HOUSE
P U B L I S H E R S
An imprint of Infobase Publishing

Brain Development

Chelsea House
An imprint of Infobase Publishing
132 West 31st Street
New York NY 10001

ISBN-10: 0-7910-8954-1
ISBN-13: 978-0-7910-8954-5

Library of Congress Cataloging-in-Publication Data
Bangalore, Lakshmi.
  Brain development / Lakshmi Bangalore.
     p. cm. — (Gray matter)
  Includes bibliographical references and index.
  ISBN 0-7910-8954-1 (hardcover)
  1. Brain—Growth—Juvenile literature. I. Title. II. Series.
  QP376.B276 2007
  612.8'2—dc22   2006032428

Chelsea House books are available at special discounts when purchased in bulk quantities for businesses, associations, institutions, or sales promotions. Please call our Special Sales Department in New York at (212) 967-8800 or (800) 322-8755.

You can find Chelsea House on the World Wide Web at http://www.chelseahouse.com

Text and cover design by Terry Mallon

Printed in the United States of America

Bang EJB 10 9 8 7 6 5 4 3 2 1

This book is printed on acid-free paper.

All links and Web addresses were checked and verified to be correct at the time of publication. Because of the dynamic nature of the Web, some addresses and links may have changed since publication and may no longer be valid.

Contents

1 Brain Basics

What makes us distinctly human? After all, we look similar to other primates. Genetically, we are nearly identical to our closest evolutionary cousin, the chimpanzee. And yet, we are the most technologically advanced species on Earth. We are able to develop complex tools, machines, and processes. We can communicate abstract thoughts and ideas using language and symbols. Such uniquely human traits are made possible by our brain—the organ that controls everything we do, from the beating of our heart to the blinking of our eyes, from seeing, feeling, and thinking to emotion, speech, and reasoning. Although our brain weighs about 3 pounds (1.4 kilograms) and makes up only about 2% of our body mass, it is strikingly larger and more complex than the brain of any other primate. As an essential component of the nervous system within us, it supports and provides a platform for information transfer, connection between organ systems, and memory storage.

BUILDING BLOCKS

Our nervous system is a vast network of billions of building blocks called **neurons.** Neurons are specialized cells that transmit messages between the brain and the rest of the body. A typical neuron has branching fibers or **dendrites** that receive messages, a **cell body** where the messages are processed, and a long wire-like transmission line called the **axon** (Figure 1.1).

1

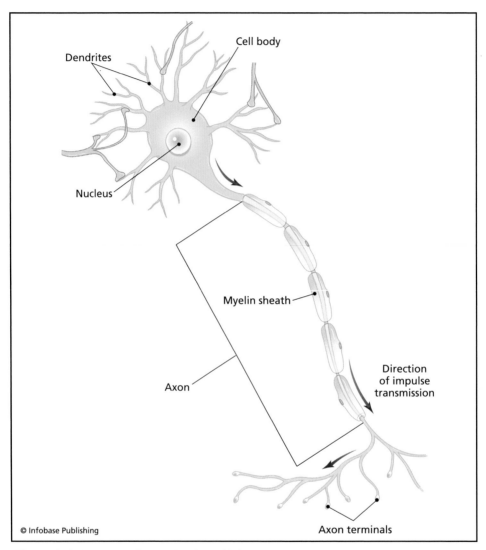

Figure 1.1 A neuron is the basic building block of our nervous system. It helps transmit messages to and from the brain.

All neurons are electrically charged relay stations. When called to action, they transmit messages in the form of brief discharges of electricity. Such discharges are referred to as nerve impulses or **action potentials**. Electrical discharge takes place

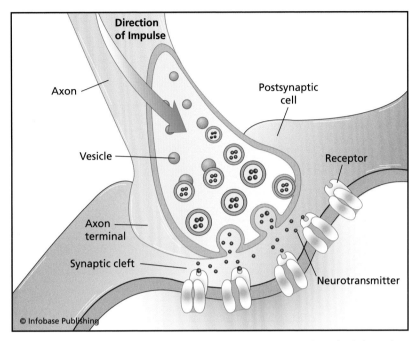

Figure 1.2 In this illustration of a synapse, an electrical impulse causes the release of neurotransmitters from vesicles within the axon terminus of a neuron. The neurotransmitters cross the synaptic cleft and bind to receptors of an adjacent neuron.

sequentially in a domino effect, beginning near the cell body, traveling along the length of the axon, and ending at the axon terminus where the impulse is relayed to the next neuron along the chain of communication.

The region where a nerve impulse is transmitted from one neuron to another is called the **synapse** (Figure 1.2). When a nerve impulse arrives at the axon terminus, it triggers the release of special chemicals called **neurotransmitters** into the synapse. Neurotransmitters help transmit messages across the synapse from the transmitting cell to the receiving cell. The **electrochemical process** is the process in which cells convert chemical signals into electrical signals, and electrical signals back to chemical signals.

Neurons that transmit impulses from sense organs—eyes, nose, skin, ears, and tongue—toward the brain and spinal cord are called sensory, or afferent, neurons. Neurons that transmit impulses away from the brain and spinal cord toward organs such as muscles and glands, are called motor, or efferent, neurons. Neurons that relay impulses between sensory and motor neurons are called **interneurons**. Some neurons can transmit impulses faster than others. Neurons such as the A-beta nerve fibers carry touch-related information to the brain and can transmit at speeds of up to 200 mph (322 kilometers per hour). On the other hand, neurons such as the C-nerve fibers that carry pain and temperature-related information to the spinal cord, transmit at much lower speeds—about 2 mph (3.22 km/h).

Neurons that are capable of high-speed transmission have a special type of insulation around their axons. This insulation, known as **myelin** (Figure 1.3), prevents leakage of action potentials as they travel down an axon's length, just like the insulation that prevents leakage of current from electrical wires. However, unlike the insulation around electrical wires, myelin is not continuous. Gaps at regular intervals called **nodes of Ranvier**, or "nodes" for short, interrupt its continuity. Specialized molecules located at the nodes ensure that nerve impulses do not wither away in their long-distance travel from one end of the axon (near the cell body) to the other (axon terminus). The presence of both myelin and nodes of Ranvier allows nerve impulses to leap from one node to another almost instantaneously. This type of impulse transmission, known as **saltatory conduction**, enables neurons to function with incredible speed and efficiency. Thanks to saltatory conduction, neurons such as those that detect a pinprick are able to relay signals so quickly that they usually produce a sharp and instantaneous response—you quickly jerk your finger away from the

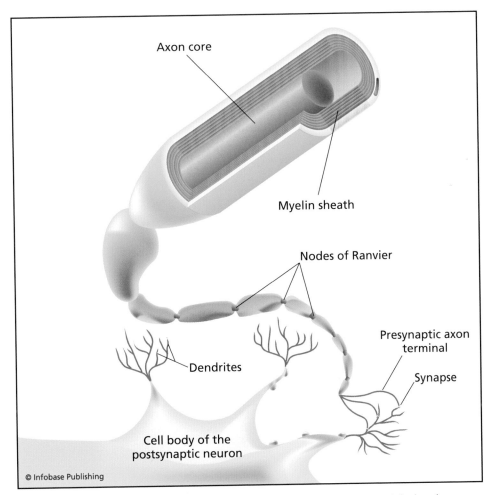

Figure 1.3 A fatty substance called myelin surrounds axons and helps increase the speed of nerve impulse transmissions. Unmyelinated gaps at regular intervals along the axon help maintain the signal intensity of nerve impulses as they travel from one end of the axon to the other.

pin. Unmyelinated sensory neurons transmit signals at a much slower rate, alerting the brain to pain that is slower in onset, dull, and more spread out.

The proper functioning of the nervous system depends on cells called **glia**. There are 10 times as many glial cells in our brain as there are neurons. Glia perform many important tasks within the nervous system. They produce the myelin that insulates axons, provide nutrients and other substances that promote neuron growth, nurse and repair neurons that are injured, and protect the nervous system from infection.

Myelin is actually an extension of the cell membrane of a glial cell. Axons with thick sheaths of myelin might have as many as 50 layers of myelin wrapped around them. Smaller diameter axons may have as few as 2 or 3 layers. **Oligodendrocytes** are the glia that produce myelin in the **central nervous system.** Glial cells called **Schwann cells** provide myelin to axons of the **peripheral nervous system,** which is made up of neurons that reside or project outside the brain and spinal cord. Myelinated regions of neurons appear white and are therefore referred to as the **white matter**. Damage to myelin occurs in diseases such as **multiple sclerosis** and in many cases of spinal cord injury. When this happens, transmission of nerve impulses is disrupted, leading to a variety of movement and sensory abnormalities such as paralysis, vision loss, slurred speech, and pain.

BRAIN STRUCTURES

The human brain can be divided into three major units. They are the **cerebrum, cerebellum,** and **brain stem,** arranged from top to bottom around the central axis of the brain stem (Figure 1.4). The brain contains a rich supply of blood vessels. The brain and its connecting blood vessels are surrounded by three layers of membranes called **meninges** and a protective sea of **cerebrospinal fluid,** and enclosed within the bony framework of the skull. Remarkably, even though the human brain makes up only about 2% of the body mass, it receives nearly 20% of the oxygen-rich blood supply with every beat of the heart. Neurons die if the blood supply to the brain is interrupted even for a few minutes. This happens, for example, in people experiencing a

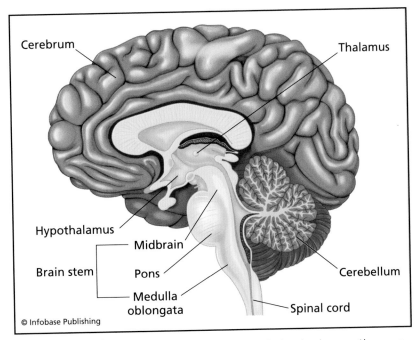

Figure 1.4 The three major components of the brain are the cerebrum, cerebellum, and brain stem. The brain stem consists of three segments: the midbrain, pons, and medulla oblongata. The thalamus serves as a relay station for information to and from the cerebrum. Just below the thalamus is the hypothalamus, which helps regulate body temperature, hunger, and thirst.

stroke, when the blockage or breaking of a blood vessel that supplies blood to the brain causes neurons to die. This can result in permanent brain damage and disability.

In evolutionary terms, the most advanced part of the human brain is the cerebrum. The intelligence of an animal depends on the size and complexity of the cerebrum. Our ability to learn through reasoning, intuition, and perception is due to this structure. It controls our conscious thoughts and voluntary movements. The highly wrinkled outer surface of the cerebrum resembles a giant walnut. It is referred to as the **cerebral cortex.**

The bumps and bulges on the cerebral cortex are called **gyri** (singular, gyrus), and the grooves are called **sulci** (singular, sulcus). The cerebral cortex is made up of cell bodies of neurons and the initial portions of their axons and dendrites. Because of its reddish gray appearance, it is also referred to as **gray matter**. A specific region within the cerebral cortex called the **motor cortex** controls voluntary movement of muscles. Another region called the **sensory cortex** processes information from the sense organs.

Just beneath the cerebral cortex is the subcortical white matter. This region of the cerebrum is responsible for information transmission. At the base of the cerebrum is a group of structures known as the **basal ganglia**—the caudate nucleus, putamen, globus pallidus, and subthalamic nucleus. The substantia nigra, which is in the midbrain, is also a part of the basal ganglia. The basal ganglia are thought to be associated with the regulation of voluntary movement and with establishing posture. In disorders such as **Parkinson's disease**, **Huntington's disease**, and **Tourette syndrome**, cellular changes in the basal ganglia lead to involuntary jerking movements of the arms and legs, twitching of facial muscles, and other abnormal movements. Deep inside the two halves, or hemispheres, of the cerebrum are the **thalamus** and the **hypothalamus**. The thalamus serves as the final relay station for nerve impulses traveling up to the cerebral cortex. It is the gateway through which information from various senses is combined and parceled out to appropriate regions within the cortex. The hypothalamus is located just below the thalamus. It plays an important role in the control of basic physical desires such as hunger, thirst, sleep, and sex. It also regulates body temperature, blood pressure, and hormone release via its control of the nearby **pituitary gland.**

The cerebellum looks like a smaller version of the cerebrum. The cerebellum is made up of the cerebellar cortex and the underlying cerebellar white matter. The cerebellum is responsible for balance and coordination. Located below the cerebral hemisphere is the brain stem, which is like the stalk of the brain. It continues down to the spinal cord. The brain stem is made up of three basic regions—midbrain, pons, and medulla oblongata. In evolutionary terms, the brain stem is the oldest part of the brain and the most primitive. It resembles almost the whole brain of a reptile. The brain stem links the brain to the spinal cord and controls basic functions such as breathing, swallowing, the beating of the heart, and digestion. The brain stem also regulates the production of hormones and serves as a major route for communication between the cerebral cortex and the spinal cord and peripheral nerves.

FUNCTIONAL SYSTEMS

The brain receives and interprets messages arriving from all parts of the body and creates responses based on prior experiences and physical needs. It controls both "lower-order" involuntary activities, and "higher-order" conscious activities that involve the cerebral cortex. The motor system—the interconnected neural pathways of the motor cortex, the cerebellum, and the basal ganglia—controls voluntary movement of muscles. These pathways eventually project into the spinal cord and then out to muscle effectors. Physical activities such as kicking a ball, playing the piano, or riding a bike depend on the motor system.

Involuntary or automatic activity of muscles, such as heartbeat, breathing, and swallowing, is controlled by neurons of the brain stem. Sometimes involuntary actions, such as simple repetitive contractions of muscles during walking, are controlled by the spinal cord alone. The sensory systems process information from the various sense organs. They include the visual system for sight, olfactory system for smell, gustatory system for taste, auditory system for hearing, and somatosensory systems for the sensation of touch and temperature. Although sensory information from the eyes, ears, and skin is routed through the thalamus to specific regions within the cerebral cortex, olfactory signals are routed to the cerebral cortex via a region called the olfactory bulb. Information pertaining to taste is routed via the brain stem to various parts of the gustatory system.

The limbic system, which includes the amygdale (singular, amygdala), hypothalamus, and hippocampus, controls basic but essential functions. Features such as the **fight-or-flight response**, heartbeat, respiration, sexual arousal, and control of emotions are controlled by the limbic system. The limbic system exerts its effects by influencing the **endocrine system** to

From Monkey to Man

During the course of human evolution, the complexity of our brain increased dramatically compared to other primates. The surface area of the brain, especially the cerebral cortex, increased more than threefold in comparison to the great apes, our closest evolutionary cousins. Cognitive skills such as tool use, language, and perception evolved, setting humans apart from other primates. Exactly how were these changes achieved at the genetic level? What does brain size have to do with thinking and intelligence?

These questions have captivated scientists for a long time. Recent studies of molecular evolution and comparative gene profiling have just begun to reveal some answers. The common lineage that gave rise to humans and chimpanzees is believed to have split some 5 to 6 million years ago. Research has shown that genes involved in brain development went through an especially fast rate of evolution in the lineage that led to humans.

secrete hormones, and also affects the autonomic nervous system, which controls involuntary movements. For example, the hypothalamus, via its connection to the pituitary gland—the master gland that controls the endocrine system—regulates drives and actions, heart rate, and respiration. The amygdala, a key player in the control of emotions, is associated with feelings such as fear, aggression, pleasure, and arousal. Rats with their amygdala removed snuggle up to cats, and monkeys with damage to their limbic system can be either tame and passive or wild and aggressive. The hippocampus plays an important role in processing information to form long-term memories. In conditions such as Alzheimer's disease, the hippocampus is one

Among the brain-specific genes that evolutionary research identified are microcephalin, ASPM, CDK5RAP2, and CENPJ. These genes were already known to control brain size. Studies have revealed that microcephalin changed most dramatically during the early stages of primate evolution, around 25 to 30 million years ago, when the lineage that would eventually give rise to chimpanzees and humans began to appear. ASPM, on the other hand, changed most dramatically later in evolution, some 5 to 6 million years ago, in the lineage that led to humans.

In modern humans, gene mutations in either microcephalin or ASPM result in a developmental disorder called microcephaly. Children born with microcephaly have smaller heads and decreased brain size, and are mentally retarded. The size of a microcephalic brain is about one-third the size of a normal human brain, and roughly comparable to the brains of early hominids.

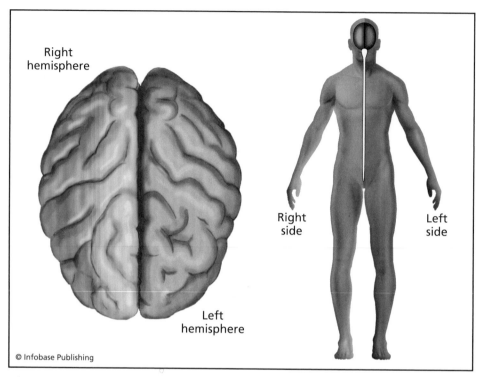

Figure 1.5 The brain is divided into left and right hemispheres. The left hemisphere controls function related to the right side of the body and the right hemisphere controls the left side of the body.

of the major regions to suffer damage resulting in symptoms such as memory problems and disorientation.

Although the brain is nearly completely divided into right and left hemispheres that appear to be built symmetrically, some functions are more strongly represented in one hemisphere than the other. Functions such as the ability to read, speak, and solve mathematical problems are more strongly represented in the left hemisphere, whereas musical and artistic creativity, and the ability to understand shapes and form are generally associated with the right brain. Another general feature of the brain is **crossed representation**, in which each side of the brain receives information about and controls function related to the opposite side of the body (Figure 1.5). For example, sensations of touch, heat, and cold from the right side of the body are processed within the **somatosensory cortex** in the left cerebral hemisphere. A major exception to the rule of crossed representation is the cerebellum. Here each cerebellar hemisphere controls coordination and muscle tone on the same side of the body.

KEY POINTS

The brain controls everything we do and feel. As an essential part of the nervous system, it functions through a network of billions of neurons. Neurons are electrically charged relay stations. They carry messages to and from the brain in the form of electrochemical signals. Sensory neurons transmit information to the brain from the various sense organs, while motor neurons transmit messages away from the brain toward various organs and muscles. The major structural units of the brain are the cerebrum, cerebellum, and brain stem. The intelligence of an animal depends on the size and complexity of the cerebrum. The cerebellum controls balance and coordination, while the brain stem controls basic instincts and feelings. The nervous system is the most complex system inside the human body.

■ **Learn more about the contents of this chapter** Search the Internet for *action potential, the human brain,* and *neurological disorder.*

2

Origins of the Nervous System

Human development begins with a single fertilized egg smaller than a grain of sand. With precision timing, guided largely by the genetic blueprint within, the fertilized egg begins its journey to develop into a complete individual with specialized cells, tissues, organs, and interconnected systems. First begins a series of cell divisions, from a single cell stage to 2, 4, 8, and so on. Within days, the raspberry-like cluster of about 16 cells leaves the fallopian tube in the female reproductive system and enters the womb. As cell divisions continue, a hollow cavity begins to form inside the rapidly expanding cell cluster. The appearance of a hollow cavity identifies the entire structure as a **blastocyst** and indicates the formation of two distinct cell types—an outer rim of trophoblasts and an inner mass of blastomeres (Figure 2.1). The trophoblasts develop into the placenta, the thin tissue that surrounds a growing fetus. The blastomeres, also known as **embryonic stem cells**, give rise to the embryo and thus to every individual cell that comes to lie within us.

IMPLANTATION

Signals released by both the trophoblasts and the ovaries (the female reproductive glands that release the egg) prepare the wall of the womb and the blastocyst for **implantation.**

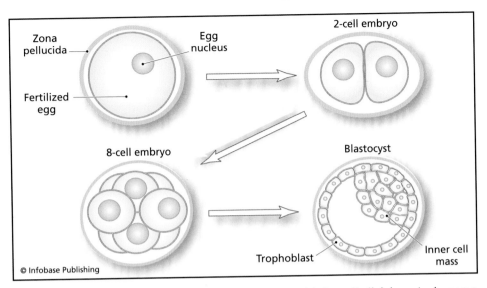

Figure 2.1 A fertilized egg (zygote) undergoes multiple cell divisions to become a blastocyst. The inner cell mass of the blastocyst then forms three distinct layers—ectoderm, mesoderm, and endoderm—that will give rise to all the different tissues of the human body.

Implantation, or the physical attachment of the blastocyst to the womb, is a key process for continuation of the pregnancy. Upon successful implantation, the spherical blastocyst flattens into a two-layered embryonic disk. This process, known as gastrulation, begins with the formation of a narrow line of cells—the **primitive streak**—along the surface of the embryonic disk. The formation of the primitive streak is accompanied by a major rearrangement of cells that transforms the two-layered disk into a three-layered structure. This is the stage when the cells are committed to different identities within the body. The organization into three layers—an outer **ectoderm,** inner **endoderm** and middle **mesoderm**—roughly corresponds to the basic organization of a human being, with the gut on the inside, epidermis on the outside, and connective tissue in between. The endoderm gives rise to the pharynx, esophagus, stomach, intestines, and associated glands. The mesoderm gives rise to the heart, bone marrow, blood, bones, muscles, and reproductive organs. The ectoderm forms the skin, and the nervous system.

Gastrulation also marks the beginning of **body-axis** formation. Three different axes—namely the lines between the head and tail, front and back, and left and right—are specified during embryonic development. Although our body plan looks symmetrical from the outside, the internal placement of our organs follows a distinct left-right asymmetry, with heart to the left, liver to the right, and stomach and spleen to the left. Many complex cellular mechanisms control the proper placement of organs within the three-dimensional space of the developing embryo.

One important regulator of the formation of a body axis is a protein called **nodal**. Its location at the nodal region of the primitive streak influences migrating cells of the mesoderm to change into specific groups of cells. In doing so, it establishes an early pattern and body axis. Members of a large family of genes called the **homeobox** genes are also known to be important regulators of body axis formation during early embryonic development. Homeobox genes determine the position where limbs and other body parts should grow. They were first discovered in laboratory studies of fruit flies when mutations in homeobox genes produced changes in the body plan of a fruit fly. Mutations in some homeobox genes result in fruit flies with legs in the place of antennae, and mutations in some others produce duplicate pairs of wings and other alterations in the body plan.

NEURAL INDUCTION

The earliest step in the formation of the nervous system is called neural induction. It begins at around 16 days after fertilization, when the embryo is barely the size of a grain of rice. During neural induction, the embryonic **neural plate** is formed and set apart from the rest of the ectoderm. The neural plate gives rise

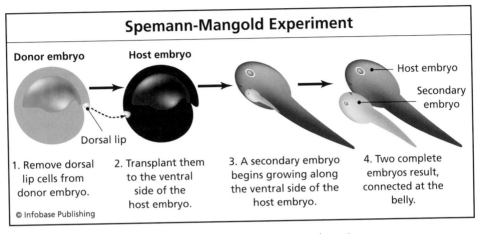

Spemann-Mangold Experiment

Donor embryo   Host embryo

Dorsal lip

Host embryo

Secondary embryo

1. Remove dorsal lip cells from donor embryo.

2. Transplant them to the ventral side of the host embryo.

3. A secondary embryo begins growing along the ventral side of the host embryo.

4. Two complete embryos result, connected at the belly.

© Infobase Publishing

Figure 2.2 Schematic of the Mangold-Spemann experiment.

to the billions of specialized neurons and glia that form the nervous system.

The idea of neural induction was first introduced in the 1920s by Hans Spemann and his student Hilde Mangold when they performed their famous "organizer experiment" using the embryos of newts in the blastocyst stage. They demonstrated that transplanting the **dorsal blastopore lip** from one embryo to the underside of another embryo results in the formation of a second nervous system (Figure 2.2). The duplicated nervous system develops not from the transplanted tissue, but from the ventral ectoderm—the region that normally gives rise to skin tissue.

This experiment demonstrated that the transplanted tissue exerts an "organizing" effect on its new environment. This means that it instructs the surrounding tissue to form a second nervous system. In the absence of such an effect, as in the case of an undisturbed embryo, the ectoderm develops into skin tissue. This suggested that the organizer, i.e., the dorsal blastopore lip, is the source of signals responsible for neural induction. The discovery of the Spemann-Mangold organizer was soon followed by the identification of equivalent regions in higher vertebrates. Each had the ability to not only induce a neural plate within the same species, but also across species, suggesting that the mechanism of neural induction is conserved among vertebrates.

The discovery by Spemann and Mangold sent scientists on a frantic search for signals released by the organizer. Although they initially assumed that there was just one signal, it became clear that more than one signal affects neural fate. The signals do so not by inducing neural fate, but by blocking the action of molecules that inhibit neural fate. Three diffusible proteins—noggin, follistatin, and chordin—were isolated from the organizer and shown to induce neural fate by blocking the action of the inhibitors of neural fate. The inhibitors of neural fate were identified as **bone morphogenetic proteins** (BMPs). Blocking of the action of BMPs by proteins noggin, follistatin, and chordin allows ectodermal cells to follow their default fate and give rise to cells and tissues of the nervous system. This, however, is only a simplistic description of the mechanisms that mediate neural induction. Scientists have yet to definitively demonstrate all the molecular requirements for the formation of the neural plate in mammals. As research on neural induction continues, new molecular players and complex cellular interactions are beginning to emerge.

FORMATION OF THE NEURAL TUBE

The earliest visible change in response to neural induction is an increase in the height of the cells destined to become parts of the nervous system. They change from being cube-shaped cells to becoming column-shaped, resulting in the formation of the neural plate. With a wider head end and a narrow tail end, the spoon-shaped sheet of cells of the neural plate is referred to as the neuroepithelium or neuroectoderm. During this time, only a

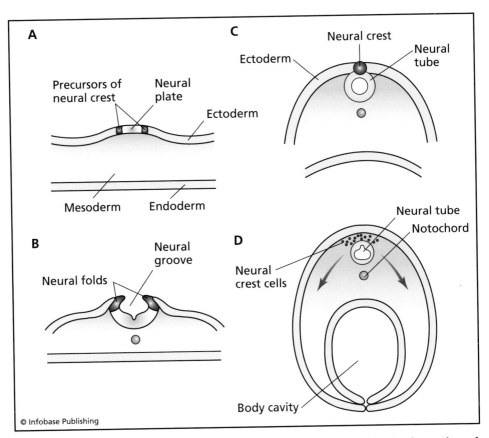

Figure 2.3 The development of the nervous system begins with the formation of the neural plate. The neural plate then folds inward to form the neural tube and the neural crest. The neural tube eventually gives rise to the brain and spinal cord, while the neural crest cells diffuse to other parts of the developing embryo and give rise to the peripheral nervous system and other body structures.

limited number of cells from the neuroectoderm are allowed to develop into neurons. If this does not happen, a grossly enlarged nervous system results, at the expense of other body tissues. This was demonstrated by experiments in fruit flies in which disruption of the process of **cell fate specification** results in embryos with a highly enlarged and abnormal nervous system. These embryos do not survive beyond the early embryonic period. A major regulator of the process of cell fate specification during development is a molecule called **Notch**. Notch mediates cell fate decisions by controlling the ability of developing cells to respond to developmental signals. In doing so, it dictates the position of each cell within a developing organ. Like many of the genes involved in development, Notch and members of the signaling cascade that it initiates are highly conserved, being structurally and functionally similar in species ranging from flies to humans.

Notch Signaling

The coordinated development of all multicellular organisms requires proper communication between cells. Such communication takes place though molecular mechanisms of signaling, which influence cell fate and behavior. The Notch signaling pathway is one mechanism of signaling that is of vital importance to the development of animal species ranging from flies to humans. Abnormal regulation of the Notch signaling pathway has been associated with many human diseases and cancers.

The Notch signaling pathway is used in several different ways to control cell fate and development. In some tissues, Notch signaling represses or "silences" specific molecules within a still uninitiated cell to prevent that cell from becoming a certain type of cell, say a neuron or a skin cell. For example, during early development as neural identities are designated to cells within the neuroectoderm, Notch signaling singles out individual candidates from a uniform cluster of cells which are all equally capable of taking on a neural identity. Loss of Notch during this time results in the formation of too many neurons

Three to four weeks after fertilization, the embryo is about a tenth of an inch long (2.5 millimeters). The changing shape and molecular properties of the cells of the neural plate cause it to elongate and buckle inward. A crease begins to form along the length of the neural plate. The crease deepens into a groove that separates the neural plate into right and left halves. The neural groove continues to deepen, causing the edges of the neural plate to curl up, move closer, and eventually fuse to form an elongated, cylindrical **neural tube** (Figure 2.3). From the neural tube emerge

at the expense of non-neuronal tissue. A grossly enlarged brain results, causing the embryo to die at a very early stage.

In other cases, Notch signaling is inductive, causing the "switching on" of molecules needed to put together an organ. For example, in the case of wing formation in fruit flies, Notch signaling activates molecules involved in the growth and formation of the wings.

The existence of the Notch pathway has been known since the identification in the early 1900s of a mutant strain of fruit fly with "notched" wings. However, it was not until the Notch gene was cloned and studied in the past 10 to 15 years that its mechanism of action began to be unraveled. Central to the Notch pathway is the Notch receptor protein. It is situated within the cell membrane, with a part outside and a part inside the cell. Like a receiving antenna, the portion of Notch outside the cell detects molecular signals from its environment and transmits them to the cell's interior. In doing so, it triggers a cascade of intracellular events that ultimately results in a change in gene expression and cell fate.

three swellings, the beginnings of the three main divisions of the brain—namely, the **forebrain, midbrain,** and **hindbrain.**

The process in which the neural plate develops into a neural tube is called neurulation. At this stage, the developing embryo contains about 125,000 cells that are growing at a staggering rate of about 250,000 per minute. The neural tube closes completely by around 30 days after fertilization. Improper closure of the tube drastically affects development of the brain and spinal cord. Anencephaly is a neural tube defect in which part of the brain never develops or is completely absent. This often results in a miscarriage. Other forms of neural tube–related defects include encephalocele, a disorder in which an infant is born with gaps in his or her skull. It is not known what causes improper closure of the neural tube, but studies have shown that inadequate intake of folic acid, a common B vitamin in the mother's diet, is a key factor in causing neural tube defects.

NEURAL CREST AND THE ORIGINS FOR THE PERIPHERAL NERVOUS SYSTEM

As the neural tube closes, a narrow zone of cells called the **neural crest** originates from cells surrounding the neural tube. The neural crest cells break away from the neural tube and migrate throughout the developing embryo. The neural crest cells eventually differentiate into the many types of neurons and glia that form the peripheral nervous system. As the neural crest cells begin to break away from the neural tube, they change their shape and molecular features from those of typical "sticky" neuroepithelial cells to those of highly migratory and mobile mesenchymal cells. Thus, accompanying this transition of the neural crest cells is a loss of cell-to-cell adhesiveness. **Cell adhesion molecules,** such as N-CAM and N-cadherin, that are typically present in the neuroepithelial cells, begin to fade away. This allows the neural crest cells to migrate and populate many regions of the early embryo. They ultimately adopt a wide variety of cell fates, from neurons and glia of the peripheral nervous system, to connective tissue, cartilage, and bone-forming cells. When neural crest cells have com-

Cephalic Disorders

Cephalic disorders are birth defects that occur because of anomalies during the very early stages of nervous system development. The term cephalic means "head" or "head end of the body." The exact cause for cephalic disorders is unknown. Scientists think that cephalic disorders are caused by factors such as inherited genes, and exposure to radiation, viral infection, or other toxins during pregnancy. Some cephalic disorders occur when the bones of the skull connect prematurely. Some others occur due to an abnormal accumulation of cerebrospinal fluid in the brain, at the expense of the cerebral hemispheres.

The cephalic disorder anencephaly, in which a major portion of the forebrain, skull, and scalp is missing, results when the cephalic end of the neural tube fails to close. Without a forebrain, babies born with anencephaly lack any cerebral function and are unable to see, hear, feel, or think. Most of these babies die within a few hours or days after birth. Other disorders of improper closure of the neural tube include iniencephaly and spina bifida. In their investigations of the causes of cephalic disorders, scientists have found that addition of folic acid to the mother's diet significantly reduces the risk of neural tube defects. The prognosis for children born with cephalic disorders depends on the severity of the condition, and the extent of abnormal brain development. Many children display a variety of neurological problems such as blindness, lack of growth, deafness, paralysis, and early death.

pleted their migrations, and differentiated into the various cell types, cell adhesion molecules often reappear on the surface of these cells.

KEY POINTS

The entire nervous system develops from the ectoderm cell layer of the early embryo. The cells of the ectoderm become broadly committed to a neural lineage through an initial process called neural induction. After this, cell-to-cell communication specifies which cells should continue on their path to a neural fate and which cells should not. As with other stages of development, formation of the early embryonic nervous system depends on the action of many opposing and cooperative signals involving multiple signaling pathways. Because of the basic role they play during development, many of these signals and signaling pathways are conserved throughout evolution. While the neural tube develops into the central nervous system, the neural crest cells give rise to the peripheral nervous system. Abnormal specification of the overall body plan, disruption of neural induction, improper specification of cell fate, or glitches during formation of the neural tube, can result in severe defects in nervous system development.

■ **Learn more about the contents of this chapter** Search the Internet for *embryonic development, Hans Spemann,* and *cell fate.*

3 Neurogenesis: Birth, Migration, and Differentiation of Neurons

With successful closing of the neural tube, dramatic changes occur within its walls. At first single layered, the wall of cells within the neural tube grows in thickness and becomes multilayered as the cells expand in number. Cell division occurs within the zone of proliferation, toward the innermost region of neural tube. From there, newly produced neurons migrate outward, far and near, grabbing onto something and then pulling the rest of the cell body along. Migrating neurons are guided to their final destinations by a complex array of molecular signals and mechanisms. Upon arriving at their destinations, neurons orient themselves within specific tissue locations. They undergo distinct changes in structure and molecular composition as they prepare to form synaptic connections within the rapidly growing nervous system. Failure of neurons to migrate to their appropriate destinations can lead to abnormalities in brain development.

BIRTH OF NEURONS

Brain development begins with a rapid multiplication of cells within the front end of the neural tube. So rapid is the multiplication that, at its height, an estimated 250,000 neurons are born each minute. This leads to the formation of three hollow regions, or vesicles, namely, the forebrain, midbrain,

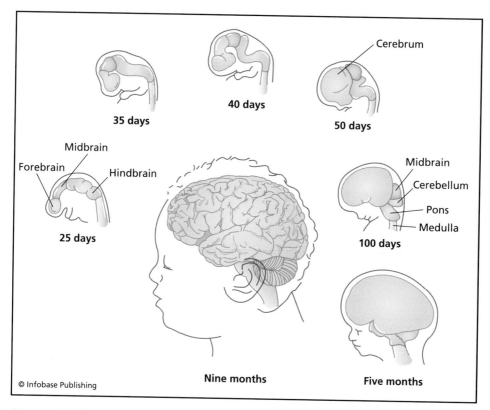

Figure 3.1 This illustration depicts the development of the human brain while inside the mother's womb. By the fourth week, the three major divisions of the brain—the forebrain, midbrain, and hindbrain—have formed.

and hindbrain, which represent the beginnings of the three major divisions of the brain (Figure 3.1). As development proceeds, each of the vesicles undergoes further growth and prepares to take on a specialized task. This growth and specialization reflects the overall architecture of the human brain. An embryonic brain with a bent, zigzag shape begins to emerge. After seven weeks of development, the forebrain becomes bigger than the midbrain and hindbrain. The forebrain eventually gives rise to the two cerebral hemispheres, including the thalamus and hypothalamus. The hindbrain corresponds to structures including the cerebellum and, together with midbrain, forms the brain stem.

As production of neurons continues, only three main structures—the cerebrum, the cerebellum, and the brain stem—are visible from the outside. The remaining structures are masked by the rapidly enlarging cerebral hemispheres. The massive expansion in cell number and the accompanying growth cause the cerebral hemispheres, which appeared smooth as ping pong balls at five months of development, to look like giant gnarled walnut halves at birth. Like trying to fit a closet's worth of clothes into a small suitcase, the surface of the expanding cerebrum folds onto itself many times, forming grooves and curves, to fit inside the fixed confines of the skull. This arrangement allows for the cerebrum to accommodate an enormous number of neurons.

Closer examination of the developing cerebral cortex reveals that the multiplication of neurons occurs at the innermost surface of the vesicle, namely the **ventricular zone** and the **subventricular zone** immediately next to the ventricular zone. In addition to the newly produced neurons, these zones of proliferation contain a population of glial cells called radial glia (Figure 3.2). These glial cells span the thickness of the developing cerebral cortex. As wave upon wave of young neurons is produced in the zones of proliferation, the **radial glia**, which look like miniature rope ladders, provide tracks for these neurons to climb outward and migrate to their respective destinations. Neurons that are born first settle into the deepest layers of the cortex while those born later migrate past the first-born neurons, farther away from the zones of proliferation. Upon reaching their destination, neurons get off the glial ladders and make way for the next wave of migratory neurons on their way to even more distant destinations. In this way, cortical neurons accumulate to form the six distinct layers of the cerebral cortex. Eventually, neurons

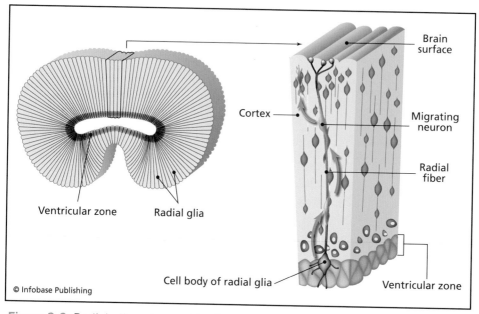

Figure 3.2 Radial glia act as guides for newly formed neurons by leading them to their final destinations in the cerebral cortex.

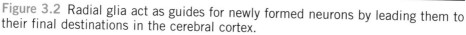

in each layer become specialized in form and function to perform their assigned roles in the brain.

Until recently, it was a long-held belief that new neurons are produced only before birth and that neurons in the adult brain can never be replaced if they are lost. Although most of the neurons in the brain are already present at the time of birth, there is now increasing evidence that the adult brain has the capacity to generate new neurons. We now know that at least two regions within the brain—the hippocampus and the olfactory bulb—produce neurons throughout the course of one's life. Current research is focused on understanding why the production of neurons, or **neurogenesis**, persists in select regions of the adult brain, and what, if any, function these newly produced neurons serve. A better understanding of the process of neurogenesis in the hippocampus and the olfactory bulb could help scientists figure out ways to use neurogenesis in the adult brain to repair the damaged central nervous system.

NEURONAL MIGRATION

Although the longest and most complex migration within the central nervous system takes place in the developing cerebral cortex, neuronal migration takes place within most structures of the developing brain. Long migratory voyages of young neurons are also seen in the case of neurons that populate the olfactory bulb—the region of the brain that receives odor signals from olfactory neurons that are present within the olfactory epithelium.

New olfactory neurons are produced throughout life. In the brains of adult mice, an estimated 12,000 neurons travel 8 millimeters (.3 inch) from the subventricular zone through the forebrain to reach their destination in the olfactory bulb. This is an amazing journey for a neuron that is only 10 to 30 micrometers (.0004 to .001 inches) in diameter. Neurons of the hippocampus, on the other hand, do not have to migrate far. They are generated in a region called the dentate gyrus, immediately next to where they are needed. Migrating neurons of the cerebral cortex rely on radial glia to reach their destinations. But scientists believe that there must be other ways of guiding neuronal migration, since neurons also migrate in regions of the brain that have no radial glia. Currently, scientists do not completely understand all the mechanisms that control neuronal migration, but they do know that migrating neurons depend on a complex array of molecular mechanisms to reach their destination. Migrating cortical neurons, for example, depend on "sticky" cell adhesion molecules to adhere to radial glia during their passage. They also depend on the presence of contractile proteins to propel them forward.

Not all neurons survive, let alone make it to their destination. Some migrating neurons die due to lack of appropriate guidance. Some fail to reach their destination because of inherent genetic mutations. Others end up where they should not. Sometimes cortical neurons fail to get off the glial ladders, which prevents the next wave of migrating neurons from moving up and outward, leading to a pileup of neurons below. This can result in structural abnormalities or missing regions within the developing brain. Although rare, more than 20 distinct human neurological syndromes are thought to involve abnormal cortical migration or layering. **Lissencephaly**, a gene-linked brain malformation characterized by a smooth (instead of folded) cerebral cortex and absence of normal convolutions, is the result of defective neuronal migration. Children born with lissencephaly have an abnormally small head, unusual facial features, muscle spasms, seizures, and severe mental retardation. They rarely survive beyond a few years of life. Similarly, in **Kallman syndrome**, neurons that produce sex hormones and neurons that sense odors fail to migrate to their proper locations. This results in underdeveloped genitalia, sterile gonads, and complete or partial loss of the ability to smell.

Still, precisely how errors in neuronal migration cause diseases remains unclear. Environmental factors can also prevent migrating neurons from reaching their proper destination. These include exposure of the developing fetus to alcohol, cocaine, viral and bacterial infections, or radiation. Studies have shown that people exposed to high levels of radiation while in the womb are born with brain defects due to abnormalities in neuronal migration. Drug and alcohol abuse during pregnancy have also been shown to have serious effects on cortical development and to result in infants with smaller head size, and difficulties in neurological functioning. The precise mechanisms by which

Brain Trek: The Journey of Neuronal Migration

Newborn neurons originate from the interior wall of the neural tube. From there, they permanently relocate and take their place within the developing brain. Young neurons must migrate far and near, from the outer reaches of the brain to structures close to their place of origin. In a journey of epic proportions, the approximately 100 billion neurons that make up the human brain must travel great distances—sometimes equivalent to a human walking from Connecticut to California—to reach their destinations. How do neurons achieve such a remarkable feat?

By examining the brains of monkeys, scientists have found that specialized cells called radial glia guide newborn neurons of the cerebral cortex in their journey. Like inchworms crawling on a pole, migrating neurons crawl along radial glia from their place of birth to points farther and farther away. Upon completion of their journey, they arrange themselves neatly in an inside-out pattern, such that the first wave of migrated neurons is closest to the place of birth, while later waves travel longer distances, winding their way past the earlier arrivals, to arrive at their destinations closer to the surface of the brain.

Scientists have found that neurons that populate the olfactory bulb use a different method of migration that does not involve the help of radial glia. These young neurons become closely associated with each other, as they migrate in long chains or aggregates. Special molecules called cell adhesion molecules also help migrating neurons along the path to their eventual destination. Scientists believe that many more molecules and mechanisms that guide neuronal migration remain to be discovered.

environmental factors disrupt neural migration also remain largely unknown.

NEURONAL DIFFERENTIATION

As newly formed neurons become mature neurons and take on specialized jobs, they change their shape, size, and molecular composition depending on the function they will perform. They become polarized and develop branches—dendrites and axons—from their cell bodies. As dendrites grow and branch out, they provide a greater surface area for axon terminals from other neurons to form synapses. The number of dendrites and the extent of branching varies from one type of neuron to the other.

The way different types of neurons acquire their distinct dendritic arbors or branches is not completely understood. Recent studies have provided some clues. A protein called Dasm1, short for "dendrite arborization and synapse maturation 1," is present in developing mouse brain. It plays an important role in dendritic arborization (branching of dendrites). Suppression of Dasm1 activity in a developing mouse brain impairs dendritic arborization, but not axon growth. Axons, on the other hand, grow in length to establish connections with other neurons, much like electrical cables extending from a main power station to neighborhoods in the area. Some axons extend locally, reaching out and connecting with other neurons nearby, while others must grow several feet in length, making their way through surrounding tissue and complex terrain to make their connections. With the formation of axons and dendrites, a typical tree-like form of the mature neuron emerges. Each neuron also goes through further specialization as it acquires distinct molecular features needed to perform specific tasks within the nervous system (Figure 3.3).

Some neurons acquire pyramid-shaped cell bodies, while others acquire smaller and rounder cell bodies. Some become

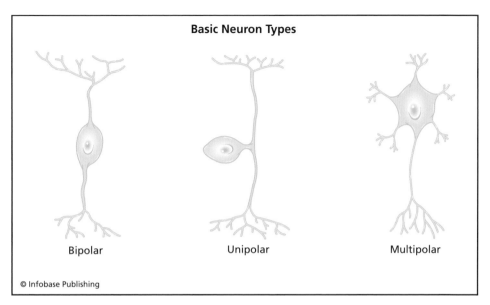

Figure 3.3 Neurons can be classified by their structural differences. Bipolar neurons consist of a single axon and a single dendrite on opposite sides of the cell body. Unipolar neurons consist of a short fiber that extends from the cell body and then branches into an axon and a dendrite. Multipolar neurons have a single axon and many dendrites, and are the most common type of neuron in the central nervous system.

motor neurons, while others become sensory neurons and interneurons. Still others become glial cells. The process of neuronal **differentiation** during development is an area of intense investigation. Studies indicate that several factors, including the location of newly formed neurons and their surrounding environment, control the type of neuron into which they will differentiate. One key factor known to regulate neuronal differentiation is a secreted protein called **sonic hedgehog** (named after a popular video game character). Sonic hedgehog operates as a positional signal. This means that sonic hedgehog has a different effect on the target cell depending on the distance that separates them. Cells immediately next to sonic hedgehog differentiate into a specialized class of glial cells. Cells farther away, and thus exposed to lower levels of sonic hedgehog, differentiate into motor neurons. Much more distant neurons exposed to even smaller concentrations of sonic hedgehog differentiate into interneurons.

Precise choreography of **gene expression** is essential for proper differentiation of neurons. Gene expression is the process

Neurodevelopmental Disorders

The accuracy with which the complex process of brain development is orchestrated is remarkable. Sometimes, however, glitches in brain development do occur and lead to a wide range of mental, physical, and emotional deficits in affected individuals. Neurodevelopmental disorders such as autism, fragile X syndrome, dyslexia, epilepsy, cerebral palsy, schizophrenia, and bipolar disorder are the result of abnormal brain development. The causes for many of these disorders are not very well understood, although both genetic and environmental factors are thought to be involved. Glitches can occur during any phase of brain development such as the birth of neurons, migration of neurons to their proper destinations, specialization of neurons for the tasks they will perform, formation of appropriate synaptic connections, and selective elimination of misplaced or improperly connected neurons. In an effort to understand what goes wrong in the brains of individuals with disorders of brain development, scientists are first trying to map out "normal" development of the brain. Advances in brain-imaging techniques, neurobiology, and genetics are helping scientists learn more about how the normal brain develops, and in turn shedding new light on what happens when something goes wrong. An improved understanding of the underlying basis for neurodevelopmental disorders may in turn lead to effective treatments and interventions.

by which a cell's gene sequence is "expressed" to achieve a certain function. Studies have identified a variety of **transcription factors**—proteins that regulate gene expression—that are required for proper differentiation of neurons. For example, a transcription factor called Math1 is required for immature neurons to differentiate into granule cells, a type of neuron within the mouse cerebellum. Mice that lack Math1 are born without cerebellar granule cells. Another protein, Pax6, which is a member of the Pax family of transcription factors, controls neuronal differentiation in response to sonic hedgehog signaling. Mouse embryos that lack Pax6 function show many defects in brain development, including failure to form eyes and nasal cavities.

KEY POINTS

The brain develops from the front end of the neural tube. Large-scale cell proliferation within this region transforms the initially single-layered, tubular structure into one with three vesicles—the forebrain, midbrain, and hindbrain—which give rise to structures of an adult brain. During this time, cell proliferation is especially pronounced in the forebrain, causing it to enlarge out of proportion to the midbrain and hindbrain. The cerebrum and structures including the hippocampus, amygdala, thalamus, and hypothalamus are derived from the forebrain. Newly produced neurons migrate outward from the zones of proliferation along the innermost region of the neural tube to their respective destinations. As they arrive at their destinations, neurons become specialized in their shape, size, and molecular composition for the function they will perform. Migration of neurons to proper locations in the developing brain is guided by a complex array of molecular signals and mechanisms.

■ Learn more about the contents of this chapter Search the Internet for *cerebral cortex, neuron types,* and *gene expression.*

4

Wiring the Brain: Growth and Guidance of Axons and Dendrites

The formation of neuronal circuits during brain development depends on proper growth and guidance of axons and dendrites to their appropriate connections. Axons extend from their cell bodies to distant locations toward their connections, and dendrites elaborate themselves (or spread) into complex branches. During this process, axons and dendrites are guided by highly specialized structures called **growth cones** that are present at their growing tips. Growth cones convert signals they detect in their surrounding environment into guided outgrowth of axons and dendrites. The types of signals they detect may be free floating molecules released by distant target sites, or molecules attached to the surface of nearby cells. Axon extension and dendrite elaboration, and their impact on biological development, are hotly investigated areas of research at this time. Although much progress has been made in understanding what contributes to guided axon extension, less is known about how dendrites acquire their distinct form and function.

THE GROWTH CONE

About 100 years ago, the famous Spanish histologist, physician, and Nobel Prize winner Santiago Ramón y Cajal recognized that the enlarged tip of growing axons is a special region where lengthening of the axon might occur. He named this region the growth cone. Although he made this observation using slices of embryonic tissue and tools that might be considered primitive to today's standards, he nevertheless set the stage for future experiments that captured striking images of advancing living growth cones. These modern images showed that the growth cone is in fact the expanding tip of an axon. New cell membrane is added at the region of the growth cone to cause axon elongation. Axons can lengthen at the rate of several millimeters per day. As the axon elongates, raw material needed for elongation is transported via specialized cargo vesicles from the cell body down to the growing tip. The growth cone influences axon elongation and steers its path by responding to guidance signals in its surrounding environment.

A typical growth cone looks like the leaf of a palm tree, with a ruffled shape and fingerlike projections called **filopodia** (Figure 4.1). Special sensors, or receptors, that line the surface of filopodia recognize **guidance molecules** on surrounding axons, cells, and the **extracellular matrix.** Upon recognizing the guidance molecules, receptors dispatch the message to the neuron's nucleus via special messenger proteins located in the growth cone's cytoplasm. Inside the nucleus, the message brings forth a change in gene expression, signaling the production or disassembly of materials required for growth cone building.

For example, the production of **cytoskeletal proteins**— structural elements within the growth cone—affects movement of the growth cone toward or away from the direction of the guidance signal. The cytoskeleton of a growth cone is made up of cytoskeletal proteins called microfilaments and microtubules, which are themselves complex molecules made of smaller units called actin and tubulin. The formation of these complex molecules, or polymers, is called polymerization. Movement of the growth cone depends on the polymerization

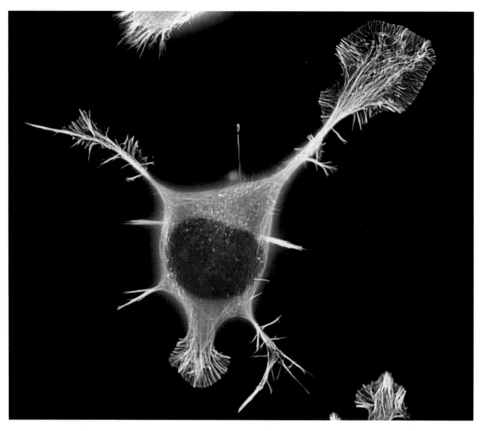

Figure 4.1 Pictured above is a fluorescent light micrograph of a cell following stimulation by nerve growth factor. The cell body contains the nucleus (purple). The initially spherical cell has formed long branch-like extensions called neurites (pink) that will grow into an axon and dendrites. Growth cones (fan-like structures) at the tips of neurites help them reach their appropriate connections.

of actin at the filopodia tips and the extension of microtubules from the central core of the growth cone. Drugs such as cyto-chalasin and colchicine, which interfere with polymerization of actin and tubulin respectively, have been shown to inhibit movement of the growth cone.

The study of growth cone guidance in humans is not feasible because of the potential risk it poses to the developing embryo. Fortunately, many of the guidance molecules and the mechanisms they use for signaling are conserved throughout evolution, which means that they look and behave the same way in species ranging from insects and worms to humans. This has made the task of studying growth cone guidance easier for scientists. They can use simpler organisms such as worms and insects in studies, and then use the results to form hypotheses about growth cone guidance during human brain development. Some of the earliest studies on growth cone guidance and axon pathfinding, as it is sometimes called, were done in grasshopper embryos. Such studies demonstrated that moving growth cones depend on molecular "signposts" to guide them through the complex terrain of the embryonic tissue. The studies also showed that growth cones consistently meander through the same path to reach their target. Later analyses of developing motor neurons in chicken embryos also confirmed that axon pathfinding is not a random process.

GUIDANCE MOLECULES

Growth cone guidance depends on the growth cone recognizing guidance molecules. There are a variety of growth cone guidance molecules. Some guidance molecules provide guidance by attraction and steering growth cones toward them, while others provide guidance by repulsion, or steering growth cones away from incorrect regions. Some guidance molecules are fixed to the surface of cells, and thus provide only short-range guidance. Other guidance molecules lay diffused in the extracellular space and are capable of providing both short- and long-range guidance to growth cones. Many guidance molecules, with names such as netrins, cadherins, semaphorins, neuropilins, ephrins and plexins, have been identified. As if the identified array of guidance molecules is not confusing enough, many of them are members of highly conserved and very large families of proteins. Yet, scientists believe that there must be many more guidance molecules, and that the current knowledge of the mechanisms that control growth cone guidance is still in its infancy. This may not be surprising, considering not only the sheer number but also the highly distinct nature of synaptic connections that billions of neurons have to make during brain development.

One group of guidance molecules is the semaphorin family, which contains more than 20 different kinds of growth molecules. The semaphorins generally guide growth cones by repelling them away from areas where they should not go. But they can provide guidance by attraction as well. Semaphorins, netrins, and slits (another kind of guidance molecule), can spread out freely in the extracellular space and act locally or at long distance. Some semaphorins are also tethered to the surface of surrounding cells. They can only act within a short range of the growth cone to which they are near. Netrins attract some growth cones and repel others. Their action is both short- and long-range. Slits are growth cone repellents, acting via a receptor that is present on the surface of some growth cones. Repulsion of the growth cone not only halts the advancing axon, but also results in the withdrawal of filopodia and shrinkage of the growth cone.

Growth cones need a surface to adhere to as they move forward. This is provided by the surface of other cells or by the extracellular matrix that surrounds them. Growth cones are able to stick to other cells with the help of molecules called cell adhesion molecules, or CAM for short. CAMs not only provide adhesive function, but also function as signaling molecules. They trigger molecular events within the growth cone to bring about a physical change in its movement and thus steer it in the proper direction. Adhesion molecules in the extracellular matrix also affect the growth of axons by providing attachment sites for growth cones. Thus, depending on the types of guidance molecules that surround the growth cone, as well as on the types of receptors that are present on the growth cone, the elongating axon is guided to its target connection during the formation of neural circuits within the developing embryo.

NEURONAL SURVIVAL

As the axon reaches the target region, the growth cone branches out to form a synapse. This is a highly specific process, called target invasion, in which the growth cone has to recognize the correct cell type within the target tissue and establish contact. The beginning stage of recognition and contact gives rise to a basic map of synaptic connections. The initial basic map is then refined by events such as cell death, branch withdrawal, and synapse elimination. Between 20% to 80% of neurons die during development, usually right around the time of target invasion. During the development of the chicken embryo, for example, about half of the 22,000 spinal motor neurons die within 5 to 7 days of neurogenesis, which is about the same time that axons reach their target cells. After this period, the number of neurons remains relatively constant.

Why do so many neurons die during the time of target invasion? In the 1920s, a neurobiologist named Victor Hamburg was studying the development of a frog spinal cord. He noted that the removal of a limb affects the survival of motor neurons within the developing nervous system. This suggested that the target tissue, the limb in this case, was making something that was needed for motor neurons to survive.

Extending this study further, neurobiologists Rita Levi-Montalcini and Stanley Cohen pinpointed the factor needed for neuronal survival, and called it nerve growth factor. These and other studies that soon followed led to the neurotrophic hypothesis, which states that neurons compete for limited quantities of **neurotrophic factors** produced by the target tissue (Figure 4.2). Neurons that get enough neurotrophic factors survive whereas the others perish (Figure 4.3).

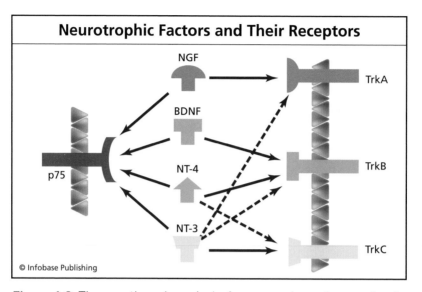

Figure 4.2 The growth and survival of neurons depends on a family of proteins called neurotrophic factors or neurotrophins. The neurotrophin family includes nerve growth factor (NGF), brain-derived neurotrophic factor (BDNF), neurotrophin 3 (NT-3), and neurotrophin 4 (NT-4). The two classes of cell surface receptors that bind to neurotrophins are p75 and Trk family. Neurotrophins and their preferred receptors are shown with bold arrows. The dashed arrows indicate weak interactions.

Although nerve growth factor was the first neurotrophic factor shown to promote neuronal survival, many others were discovered later. Each supports the survival of distinct groups of neurons. For example, one neurotrophic factor known as neurotrophin 3 supports the survival of neurons that bring sensory information into the brain and spinal cord.

Thus more neurons are produced than can be maintained, and more axons invade target areas than are necessary. Neurotrophic factors control the naturally occurring death of excess neurons during embryonic development. This ensures that the number of surviving neurons matches the size of the targets that they invade. Scientists continue to study neurotrophic factors and

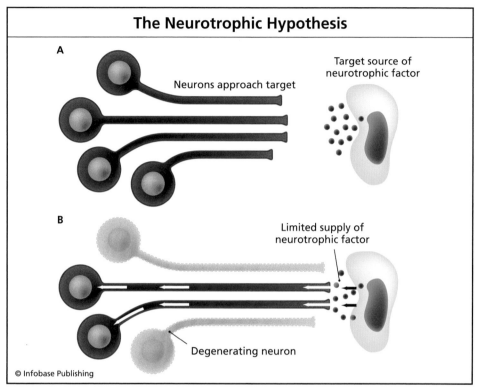

The Neurotrophic Hypothesis

A
Neurons approach target

Target source of
neurotrophic factor

B
Limited supply of
neurotrophic factor

Degenerating neuron

© Infobase Publishing

Figure 4.3 Neurons compete for limiting amounts of neurotrophic factors released by the target cells. Neurons that get enough neurotrophic factors survive whereas the others die.

their effect on various types of neurons with the hope of rescuing dying neurons in devastating disorders such as Alzheimer's disease, Parkinson's disease, and Lou Gehrig's disease. Some neurotrophic factors are already being studied in human clinical trials for the treatment of Lou Gehrig's disease.

KEY POINTS

The precise wiring of neuronal circuitry during development depends on proper growth and guidance of axons and dendrites to their correct targets. Growth cones are specialized structures at the growing tips of axons and dendrites. Growth cones are equipped with molecular sensors to detect a variety of guidance molecules, which help guide axons to their appropriate synaptic targets and establish connections within the neural circuitry. When an axon reaches its target region, the growth cone branches out and invades the area to form synapses. Target invasion is a highly specific process in which the growth cone recognizes the correct cell type within the target tissue and establishes contact within it. Target cells release trophic factors that are necessary for the continued survival of the neurons. Neurons that are able to get enough trophic factors survive, while the others die.

■ **Learn more about the contents of this chapter** Search the Internet for *Santiago Ramón y Cajal*, *Rita Levi-Montalcini*, and *nerve growth factor.*

5 Network Connectivity: Formation and Strengthening of Synapses

No matter how well the birth, migration, and differentiation of neurons are choreographed, the human brain cannot function unless proper connections are made between neurons and their target cells. In fact, as discussed earlier, the life of a neuron depends on synaptic connections with and the nourishment supplied by its target. Synapse formation is a gradual process during which the surface of the advancing growth cone, or **presynaptic** axon terminal, gets very close to the **postsynaptic** cell (the next cell in the neuron chain). The initial contact is stabilized through bi-directional communication between the pre- and postsynaptic partners resulting in the formation of a mature synapse capable of efficient transfer of information between the neuron and its target. With the formation of synapses, the nervous system begins to function.

SYNAPSE FORMATION

There are an estimated 100 billion neurons within the human brain, and an even greater number of synaptic connections. A single neuron can make as many as a thousand synapses. The synapse serves as a junction for signal communication between a neuron and its target cell. It consists of the presynaptic nerve terminal, the immediately adjacent region of the postsynaptic cell, and a gap called the **synaptic cleft**, which separates the two. The synaptic cleft is microscopic, less than a millionth of an inch. The narrowness of the cleft allows signaling molecules known as neurotransmitters to quickly diffuse from the presynaptic nerve terminal to receptors on the postsynaptic cell surface. The postsynaptic cell surface can be that of a dendrite, the cell body of another neuron, or any part of a non-neuronal cell such as a muscle cell or a gland cell. Neurotransmitters are potent molecules produced by the presynaptic neurons. Some neurotransmitters excite the postsynaptic cells that receive them, while others inhibit postsynaptic cells. For example, some neurotransmitters cause excitation of heart muscle cells leading to an increase in blood pressure and heart rate. Inhibitory neurotransmitters on the other hand would have an opposite effect, serving to regulate or turn off such excitability.

Much of what we know about how synapses form comes from the study of the **neuromuscular junction**—the synapse between a motor neuron and a muscle cell (Figures 5.1 and 5.2). This peripheral nervous system synapse is a particularly good model to study synapse formation because it is relatively simple, large, and easily accessible to experimentation. Studies of the neuromuscular junction have shown that preparation for synapse formation begins with the release of a neurotransmitter called **acetylcholine** (ACh) by the advancing growth cone of a motor neuron even before it reaches the muscle cell. Meanwhile, receptors for ACh that are present all over the surface of the muscle cell begin to redistribute themselves, clustering toward the area adjacent to the arriving growth cone. This leads to a dramatic increase in the density of ACh receptors on the muscle cell at the region of the newly forming synapse. The clustering of ACh receptors on the postsynaptic region of the muscle cell is an indication of the events that will follow in the formation of a mature neuromuscular synapse.

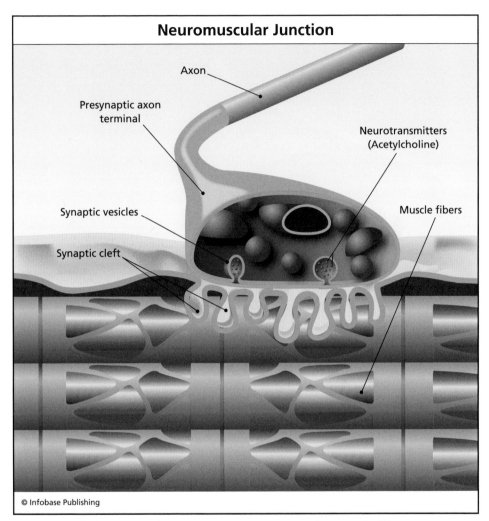

Figure 5.1 This synapse between a motor neuron and a muscle fiber causes muscles to contract. The neurotransmitter acetylcholine contained within the synaptic vesicles is released by the neuron into the synapse to act upon the muscle fiber.

SYNAPSE ELIMINATION

When a growth cone reaches its target tissue, it spreads its terminal branches over a wide surface of the target tissue and makes synapses with such energy that a huge excess of synaptic

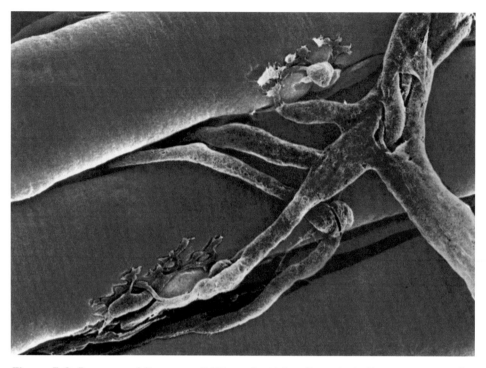

Figure 5.2 Because of its accessibility, scientists often study the neuromuscular junction to learn more about how synapses are formed. At this junction, a motor nerve (purple) interacts with muscle fibers (red) to produce a muscular response, such as contracting or relaxing.

connections is produced. At the peak of such exuberance, synapses are produced at the rate of about 2 million per second. But these immature synapses lack strength and precision. As development proceeds and synapses strengthen and mature, excess or weak synapses are removed as part of a natural process of synapse elimination called "synaptic pruning." Like removing weak branches to strengthen a tree, elimination of excess synapses reduces the overall spread of branching axons, while increasing the strength and stability of the remaining synapses. This enables the neuron to channel its energies into stronger growth and connections with fewer postsynaptic cells than before.

Because of such pruning and refining of neural connections, the 1,000 trillion or so synapses present in young children are trimmed to a mere 100 trillion to 500 trillion by adulthood.

Whether a synapse is maintained or not is determined by the level of activity within the synapse. During prenatal development, synaptic activity comes from spontaneously generated waves of nerve impulses. After birth, synaptic activity depends on sensory input from the environment. Such input, which includes visual stimulation, sound, touch, and so on, activates corresponding neurons to fire nerve impulses that converge on a postsynaptic cell. This is why, as studies have shown, babies who receive no attention from their parents may grow up with learning difficulties. Synapses between cells that work together are strengthened, whereas synapses between cells that are out of synchrony will be lost. Fifty years ago, Canadian psychologist Donald Hebb hypothesized such a mechanism, in which "neurons that fire together wire together." This mechanism forms the basis for sustained connections within the developing brain. Synapse refinement and stabilization occurs during well-defined windows of opportunity referred to as the *critical period* or the *sensitive period.* It varies for different regions of the developing brain. During critical periods, specific neural centers are especially receptive to incoming stimulation. In the presence of appropriate stimuli, they flourish, strengthening and fine-tuning their synaptic connections.

Once again, because it is simple and easy to access, the neuromuscular junction has been used extensively to study how synapse elimination works. These studies showed that during the development of a neuromuscular junction, a single embryonic muscle fiber is connected to multiple motor neurons. After birth, as development proceeds, the terminals of all but one axon begin to retract. Each muscle fiber is then connected to just a single motor neuron. This change from multiple connections to a single connection occurs gradually during the course of several weeks, when the input from one axon becomes progressively stronger. Using fluorescent dyes, and sensitive techniques, scientists have been able to track the distribution of ACh receptors in the developing neuromuscular junction. They have been able to link its distribution with the activity of a given synapse

Synapse Formation in the Brain

Although much is known about how synapses form in the peripheral nervous system, the mechanisms that guide synapse formation in the brain are currently not very well understood. This is partly because developing central nervous system neurons are more difficult to manipulate in a laboratory dish and form seemingly more complex synapses than those formed within the peripheral nervous system. Multiple connections to a target cell by more than one type of neuron, and multiple types of inputs via both excitatory and inhibitory neurotransmitters, are of common occurrence in synapses of the central nervous system. This makes it difficult to analyze not only the nature of incoming signals to the target neuron but also the requirements for initiation of synapse formation, namely the generation of the correct type of neurotransmitter receptors at correct locations along the postsynaptic target cell membrane. Despite these challenges, scientists are continuing to investigate the formation of central synapses. A better understanding of how synapses are formed in the central nervous system could identify ways to reintegrate disconnected axons into the neuronal circuitry following injuries to the brain and spinal cord. It could also suggest ways to prevent and treat diseases such as epilepsy and Alzheimer's disease, which display abnormal synaptic connectivity and function.

and its eventual fate. Such studies revealed that neuromuscular synapse elimination begins with the loss of ACh receptors on the postsynaptic cells in the area. This affects the relative ability of axons to activate their postsynaptic partners and results in the withdrawal of ineffective axon terminals.

Although there is clear evidence that synapse elimination occurs both in the peripheral nervous system and in the central nervous system, the answer to what controls synapse elimination in the central nervous system remains unclear. Studies have shown that activation of the **N-methyl-D-aspartate (NMDA)** receptors is needed for survival of synapses in the brain. Synapse elimination has been demonstrated in the visual system when **thalamocortical axons** withdraw from cells of the cortical layer IV in an activity-dependent manner. Similarly, surplus axons, which synapse with Purkinje cells in the cerebellum, disconnect during postnatal brain development until each Purkinje cell is innervated only by a single nerve fiber. Blockade of NMDA receptors in rodents during the critical period of postnatal day 15 and 16, but not before or after this period, prevents synapse elimination and leads to a permanent loss of motor coordination. These types of studies provide evidence that synapse elimination within the nervous system is an activity-dependent process that works specifically within a critical time frame of development.

KEY POINTS

Network connectivity within the developing nervous system is achieved through synapse formation. The synapse is a highly specialized region where nerve impulses are transferred from a neuron to its target cell. Synapse formation between a motor neuron and a muscle has been studied most extensively. During the formation of the neuromuscular synapse, molecules released by the neuron start a cascade of events that lead to the firing of a nerve impulse by the target cell. Although the process of synapse formation in the brain appears to be more complex than in the peripheral nervous system, scientists think that it may follow a similar sequence of events as in the peripheral nervous system. Synapse formation is often accompanied by synapse refinement in which excess, unwanted, or inappropriate connections are eliminated. Such refinement takes place during critical periods of development in an activity-dependent manner. Thus, although prenatal wiring of the neural circuitry is genetically controlled, environmental input is vital for the continued refinement and stabilization of the synapses.

■ **Learn more about the contents of this chapter** Search the Internet for *neurotransmitters*, *synaptic pruning*, and *neuromuscular junction*.

Laying the Insulation: Glia and Myelination

Another important event that greatly contributes to brain development is myelination. Myelination is a process by which glial cells systematically wrap axons in layers of fatty cell membrane known as myelin. Like the insulation that surrounds electrical wires, myelin insulates axons and prevents the loss of electrical current, while increasing the speed of impulse transmission. Myelinated axons transmit impulses faster than nonmyelinated axons of the same diameter. Speeds range anywhere from 3 feet to 300 feet per second (0.9 meters to 9 meters per second). Although the process of myelination begins as early as the fifth month of prenatal development and continues throughout life, the most rapid period of myelination occurs during the first two years after birth. Myelination of axonal pathways is largely automatic and follows a very predictable course. The timing of myelination is so precise that the stage of human development can be determined simply by examining the extent of myelination.

OLIGODENDROCYTES

The glial cells that myelinate central nervous system axons are known as oligodendrocytes (Figure 6.1). Oligodendrocytes share a common ancestry with neurons, in that they originate from the same pool of neural stem cells. Their production

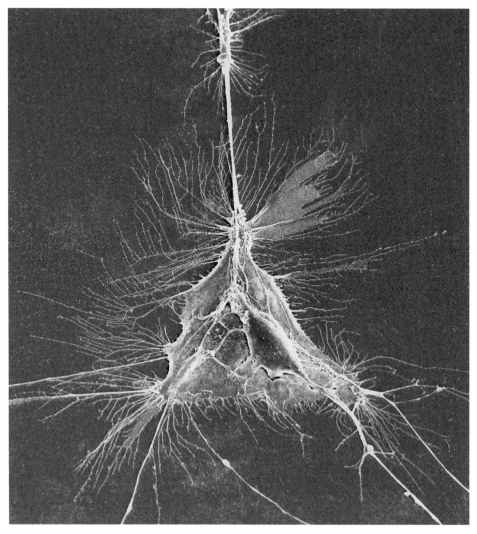

Figure 6.1 Oligodendrocytes produce an insulating material called myelin around axons of the central nervous system. A single oligodendrocyte can myelinate many axons. Above is a scanning electron micrograph of an oligodendrocyte.

begins shortly after neurogenesis when most of the neurons have taken their place in the developing nervous system. During this time a variety of signaling molecules and growth factors steer neural stem cells into a glial pathway, gradually restricting them toward becoming **oligodendrocyte precursors.** These precursors eventually give rise to mature oligodendrocytes capable of myelination. The protein sonic hedgehog is one of the key signals that control the production of oligodendrocytes from the pool of neural stem cells. Studies have shown that the removal of sonic hedgehog prevents oligodendrocyte precursors from being generated. On the other hand, application of additional sonic hedgehog leads to the formation of more oligodendrocyte precursors. Another factor, a cell surface receptor known as neuregulin, is thought to also play a role in creating oligodendrocytes. Mice lacking neuregulin fail to develop oligodendrocytes.

When the population of oligodendrocyte precursors expands to sufficient numbers—usually at the time of birth—they migrate through the developing central nervous system in search of neurons destined to be myelinated. As they make contact with axons of their target neurons, they begin to turn into mature oligodendrocytes. They stop dividing and start producing myelin-specific proteins and fats. They extend many branch-like structures in preparation for wrapping the axons. A single oligodendrocyte can extend as many as 50 to 60 branch-like structures that end in sheets of myelin membrane and is able to myelinate a variety of axons in its area.

The two most important protein components of the myelin membrane are **proteolipid protein** (PLP) and **myelin basic protein** (MBP). Mutations in proteolipid protein causes a disorder called **Pelizaeus-Merzbacher disease**, in which coordination, motor abilities, and intellectual function within the affected individual gradually deteriorates. Nearly 30 different mutations in the gene coding for proteolipid protein have been identified in humans so far, with the disease severity ranging from onset at infancy and early death, to adult-onset paralysis. Another disorder called 18q-syndrome results from the deletion of a portion of chromosome 18 that includes the MBP gene.

People with this syndrome also exhibit a gradual loss in mental and physical abilities. Both Pelizaeus-Merzbacher disease and 18q-syndrome belong to a larger group of genetic disorders known as leukodystrophies. These disorders are characterized by defective myelination and a progressive decline in the mental and physical development of an infant or a child who is born apparently normal.

The insulating ability of myelin is largely due to its high fat and low water content. Myelin is about 70% fat and 30% protein, unlike other cellular membranes which have a much lower fat to protein ratio. However, the types of fat present within the myelin membrane, namely **cholesterol**, **phospholipids**, and **glycolipids**, are similar to those in all other cellular membranes. The production of fats required to build the myelin membrane involves activation of numerous proteins. Abnormalities in proteins related to fat production or transport of fats to their correct locations within the oligodendrocytes can also result in abnormal myelin formation.

LAYING THE INSULATION

The process of myelination depends on close cooperation between target neurons and myelinating oligodendrocytes (Figure 6.2). During this time, large amounts of proteins and fats are redistributed along the oligodendrocyte membrane. Distinct regions for myelination become specified. The formation of myelin begins as sheetlike extensions of oligodendrocyte cell membrane reach out and wrap axons several times to form a tight spiral. As this happens, the material inside the extensions get squeezed out, leaving behind compacted stacks of cell membrane around the axon core. The wrapping of myelin is not continuous along the axon's length. Instead, myelination is interrupted by gaps, or bare sections called nodes of Ranvier.

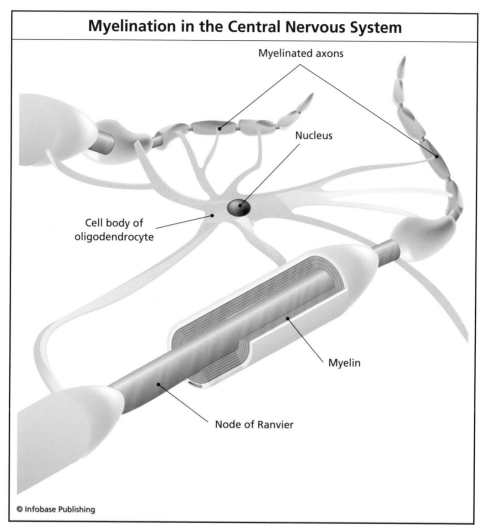

Myelination in the Central Nervous System

Myelinated axons

Nucleus

Cell body of
oligodendrocyte

Myelin

Node of Ranvier

© Infobase Publishing

Figure 6.2 An oligodendrocyte extends many branches which contact and spiral around axons to form myelin.

Special molecular cues direct oligodendrocytes to selectively wrap myelin only around axon segments between the nodes of Ranvier. The myelinated segments between the nodes of

Ranvier, which range in length from about 50 to 750 micrometers (0.002-0.03 inches) are referred to as **internodes.**

Not all axons are destined to be myelinated. In the central nervous system, the only neurons that are myelinated are those with an axon diameter of greater than 0.25 micrometers (0.00001 inches). The diameter of an axon also determines the thickness of myelin—meaning, the number of myelin wraps that surround an axon. Axons with the largest diameter, such as those of motor neurons whose function requires high-speed transmission of impulses, are the first to be myelinated. They are also the ones that have thicker myelin. Thus, myelination requires the remarkable ability of oligodendrocytes to recognize when, where, and which axons to myelinate.

The precise mechanisms or signals that regulate myelination continue to be actively investigated. Many studies have suggested the involvement of signaling between oligodendrocytes and axons. Some of this signaling involves the participation of Notch protein. Notch protein, which controls neural development by temporarily switching off the ability of a cell to respond to differentiation cues, is also present on the surface of oligodendrocytes and their precursors. The trigger for Notch, **Jagged**, is present on axons awaiting myelination. Scientists believe that the Notch signaling pathway controls the timing of oligodendrocyte differentiation and myelination because of a strong relationship between decline in Jagged expression and the start of myelination. This suggests that the presence of Jagged signals Notch to prevent oligodendrocyte precursors from growing up into mature oligodendrocytes. When the time is right, Jagged fades away, signaling the start of oligodendrocyte differentiation and myelination.

NODES OF RANVIER AND IMPULSE CONDUCTION

The basis of communication within the nervous system depends on the fact that all neurons are **polarized** (electrically charged) in their resting state. When called into action, neurons conduct nerve impulses through a wave of **depolarization** or electric discharge. The electric discharge, also known as action potential, begins near the cell body and travels, like a wave or the domino-effect, along the length of the axon to the

A Closer Look at the Node of Ranvier

The node of Ranvier is a patch of electrically excitable membrane less than 2 millimeters (.08 inches) in length. It is present at regular intervals along myelinated axons. The node of Ranvier serves as a place for traveling action potentials to become rejuvenated so that they do not wither away during their journey from one end of the axon to the other. Many specialized molecules are present at the node of Ranvier to ensure rapid regeneration of action potentials such that they can travel at speeds ranging from 0.1 to 100 meters (4 inches to 4,000 inches) per second. Most abundant among the specialized molecules at the nodal membrane are voltage-gated sodium channels. These proteins form tiny pores or gates through which sodium ions enter and exit the axon. When called to duty, sodium channels open their gates and allow sodium ions from the outside to pass into the axon. This leads to a depolarization of the axon membrane, a discharge of electricity also known as an action potential. The node of Ranvier was discovered in the nineteenth century by a French physician and pathologist named Louis Antoine Ranvier.

axon's terminus. The generation and transmission of action potentials depends on the coordinated opening and closing of special gate-like proteins called voltage-gated sodium channels that dot the axonal cell membrane. In axons that lack myelin, action potentials travel from one patch of the axonal membrane to the next in a slow and continuous manner. This type of impulse conduction is not very efficient because of the possible leakage of the traveling action potentials (electric current) along their journey. In myelinated axons, which cannot afford to lower their speed of transmission, the presence of myelin along their internodes and large clusters of sodium

Schwann Cells

Schwann cells are glial cells that insulate axons of the peripheral nervous system. They take their name from Theodore Schwann, a German physiologist and histologist who discovered them during the 1800s. Like oligodendrocytes in the central nervous system, Schwann cells wrap their cell membranes around peripheral axons through the extrusion of cytoplasmic contents and formation of compacted spiral sheaths of myelin. Myelin produced by Schwann cells, like myelin produced by oligodendrocytes, ensures speedy and efficient transmission of nerve impulses via saltatory conduction.

Schwann cells originate mainly from progenitor cells of the neural crest. The proliferation, survival, and differentiation of Schwann cells depends on a close collaboration with axons. Such collaboration takes place through a variety of factors, key among which are members of the neuregulin family of molecules produced by adjacent neurons. The dependence of channels at their nodes of Ranvier allows action potentials to be regenerated only at the nodes, thereby reducing the amount of time it takes for an action potential to reach the axon terminus. This type of impulse conduction, in which action potentials jump rapidly from one node of Ranvier to the other, is known as saltatory conduction.

Voltage-gated sodium channels work by controlling the flow of sodium ions into the axon. As the channels open their gates, a flood of sodium ions enters the axon, causing depolarization of that region of the axon membrane. An action potential is generated. It then travels to the next available region that can

Schwann cells on neuregulins has been demonstrated in laboratory studies, such as the rescue of dying Schwann cells by neuregulins and reduced Schwann cell count in mice lacking neuregulin. Schwann cells, in turn, also have a profound effect on the well being of neurons. They are known to produce a variety of molecules that not only ensure survival of neurons during development but also play an important role in regeneration of axons following peripheral nerve injury.

A characteristic feature of peripheral myelination is that each Schwann cell myelinates one axon, unlike central myelination in which oligodendrocytes typically myelinate many axons at a time. Mutations that disrupt interaction between axons and Schwann cells result in neurological disorders such as Charcot-Marie-Tooth disease, in which affected individuals gradually lose sensation and function in their extremities.

be depolarized (an adjacent unmyelinated region or the next node of Ranvier). Thus, sodium channels, in essence, behave like molecular batteries in the generation and transmission of action potentials. Like the selection of commercial batteries available for different purposes, there are many types of sodium channels. Some sodium channels open their gates at the slightest nudge, some are slow to respond, and some are eager to switch off, while some others open and close very rapidly. The precise combination of sodium channels within a neuron determines how that neuron responds to and relays nerve impulses—whether at lightning speeds, or at a snail's pace, or somewhere in between. Such a mechanism ensures that we are able to respond appropriately to different situations such as a little scrape to the knee or a dangerous situation in which we must react quickly.

LOSS OF INSULATION

Just as an electric current flowing through a wire with frayed insulation becomes short-circuited, impulse conduction along axons with damaged myelin can slow down, become distorted, or be completely blocked. With neither the insulation of myelin nor the presence of sodium channels in the bared internodes, action potentials fail to be generated or complete their journey. Nerve impulse transmission becomes blocked. This can result in a variety of neurological disabilities such as blindness, paralysis, loss of bladder and bowel control, and decline in cognitive function, depending on the extent of myelin loss. Sometimes, axons try to adapt by redistributing their sodium channels to the barren internodal membrane, restoring function, at least partially or temporarily. However, many other factors, including the presence of proteins such as potassium channels, hinder action potential conduction in demyelinated axons. Loss of myelin, or demyelination, occurs in patients with disorders such as multiple sclerosis (Figure 6.3), transverse myelitis, and spinal cord injury, as well as in hereditary diseases such as leukodystrophies. There is, as yet, no cure for damage caused by myelin loss.

Scientists are currently studying a variety of strategies from **gene therapy** to **cell transplantation**, and delivery of **growth factors** and signaling molecules, not only to prevent or minimize myelin loss, but also to stimulate remyelination in the central nervous system. Gene therapy studies of shiverer mice (which develop severe tremors because of defective myelination due to a partial deletion of the gene for MBP) have shown that supplying a normal copy of the MBP gene can lessen some of the disease symptoms. Cell transplantation studies in animal models, using a variety of myelin-forming cells such as myelinating cells from the peripheral nervous system, stems cells from bone marrow, and oligodendrocyte precursors, have shown that it is possible to restore myelin and impulse transmission in demyelinated axons of the central nervous system. Growth factors that are known to affect the production, survival, and migration of oligodendrocyte precursors are also being investigated for their potential to induce remyelination. Scientists are also investigating ways to redistribute sodium channels to demyelinated internodes as a way to restore impulse transmission. At this time, it is unclear which, if any, of these treatments or strategies will translate into cures for people with demyelination-related disorders. It is likely that a combination of therapies will ultimately provide the answer.

KEY POINTS

Myelination is an important milestone during brain development. Like the insulation that surrounds electrical wires, myelin allows fast and efficient transfer of nerve impulses to

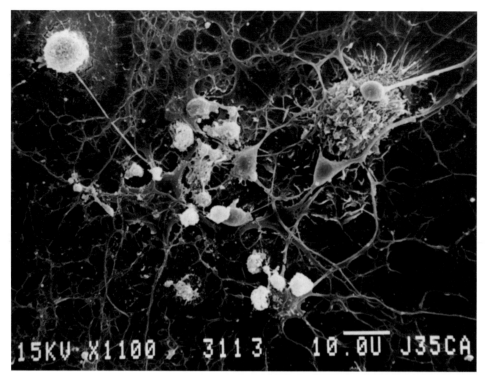

15KV X1100   311 3   10.0U J35CA

Figure 6.3 Oligodendrocytes that are overtaken by microglial cells result in demyelination. In this scanning electron micrograph, the pale, irregular microglia consume the smooth, branching oligodendrocytes, a behavior that takes place in individuals with multiple sclerosis. Demyelination causes speech and vision defects, loss of balance, and paralysis.

and from the brain. Nerve impulses travel roughly 10 times faster in myelinated axons than in unmyelinated axons of the same size. The cells that produce myelin in the central nervous system are specialized glia known as oligodendrocytes. Myelin is produced as a fatty and compressed extension of oligodendrocytes. Together with the highly excitable regions called nodes of Ranvier, myelin allows impulses to jump from node to node, down the length of the myelination at very high speeds. Factors that interfere with the production of myelin, or the migration and differentiation of oligodendrocytes, can have a drastic effect on brain development.

■ **Learn more about the contents of this chapter** Search the Internet for *nodes of Ranvier, multiple sclerosis and myelin,* and *gene therapy.*

7 The Adaptive Brain: Neural Plasticity

The genes we inherit cause our brain to develop in a certain way. However, brain development is not just the passive unfolding of a series of steps determined by our genes. It is also a continuous adaptation to the world around us. Nurture—the people around us, the experiences we undergo, the food we eat, and even the air we breathe—influences brain development in important ways. The ability of the brain to reorganize in response to its environment is called **neural plasticity**. We can see this everyday as we learn a new skill, recall an old experience, adapt to a loss, or recover from an injury. Although neural plasticity occurs throughout development, the degree which it can occur varies from birth through childhood and maturity. The basic mechanisms that are thought to support neural plasticity include the formation and elimination of synapses, continued production of new neurons in some regions of the brain, activity-dependent reorganization of neural connections, and selective elimination of neurons.

EARLY POSTNATAL PLASTICITY

The brain of a newborn baby grows and changes rapidly (Figure 7.1). One of the striking features of early postnatal brain development is the speed with which synapses are

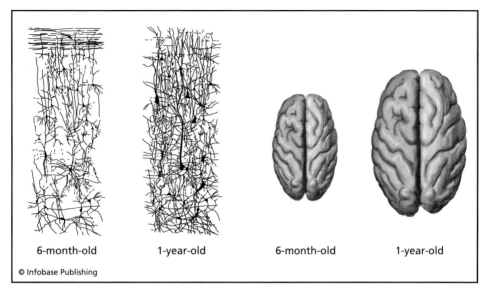

| 6-month-old | 1-year-old | 6-month-old | 1-year-old |

© Infobase Publishing

Figure 7.1 Axons and dendrites grow very rapidly during the first year of life with simultaneous increase in brain size.

formed. Having migrated to their proper locations in the brain, neurons in a developing newborn make synapses with such intensity that by 2 years of age, the brain of a typical toddler contains more than 100 trillion synapses—twice as many as in the adult brain. It is estimated that, at the peak of synapse formation, neural connections are made at a rate of about 2 million per second. Much of what we know about early post-natal plasticity comes from studies of the **primary visual cortex**, whose development is shaped by visual experience during the first few months of life. The primary visual cortex is a region of the cerebrum that is responsible for processing visual information gathered by the eyes. It consists of columns of neurons, in which each column responds best to visual input from one of the two eyes in an alternating pattern. For example, the column of neurons receiving input from the right eye is bordered by the column of neurons receiving input from the left eye. This preference of neurons for stimulation from one eye or the other is called **ocular dominance.** Each column of such neurons is referred to as the ocular dominance column.

Ocular dominance is a well-studied phenomenon that has been used to show the extent to which neural circuitry and its functions can be shaped by environmental influences. Nobel Prize–winning experiments performed in the 1960s by two researchers, Torsten Wiesel and David Hubel, showed that depriving newborn kittens the use of one eye results in reorganization of neural circuitry within the visual cortex. The result of the reorganization is that the ocular dominance columns receiving input from the nondeprived eye simply take over the areas that would normally receive input from the deprived eye. In other words, neurons deprived of stimulation from one eye are reassigned to receive input from the nondeprived eye (Figure 7.2). Such neurons synapse with neurons that bring visual input from the nondeprived eye. By varying the time and duration of visual deprivation, the researchers also showed the existence of periods that are critical for the formation of neural connections. If visual stimulation was not provided during the critical period for the formation of **visual circuitry**, the kitten would become permanently blind in the deprived eye but could see perfectly well with the eye that was left open. These landmark studies demonstrated that experience shapes neural circuitry in the developing brain. They also opened the door to our understanding and treatment of childhood cataracts and strabismus, conditions that can seriously affect visual development if they are not corrected in a timely manner.

Just as the earliest weeks and months of a baby's life are crucial for establishing neural circuits within the visual system, other cortical functions such as touch, hearing, emotion, and memory also undergo critical periods of development. Touch

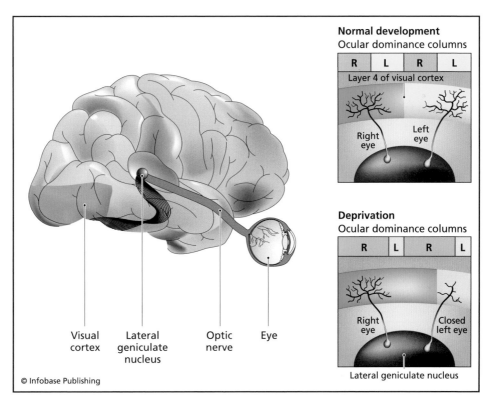

Normal development
Ocular dominance columns

| R | L | R | L |

Layer 4 of visual cortex

Right
eye

Left
eye

Deprivation
Ocular dominance columns

| R | L | R | L |

Right
eye

Closed
left eye

Lateral geniculate nucleus

Visual
cortex

Lateral
geniculate
nucleus

Optic
nerve

Eye

© Infobase Publishing

Figure 7.2 Visual deprivation of one eye leads to expansion of the ocular dominance columns that respond to the open eye at the expense of the columns that would normally respond to the blocked eye.

is not only comforting to an infant but is vital to the formation of "**touch circuits**" within the developing brain. The sense of touch depends on proper wiring between touch receptors in the skin and neurons in the sensory cortex. Laboratory studies have shown that if the whiskers of newborn rodents are clipped early in life, they never develop the neural circuitry required for receiving sensory signals from that part of the face. However, if the whiskers are clipped after the critical period for formation of touch circuits, they simply grow back and retain sensation in that area.

PLASTICITY OF LEARNING AND MEMORY

A newborn baby does not know the alphabet, let alone how to play the piano or tell time. Such skills are the result of learning and memory—two of the most fundamental processes that govern our lives. Learning (the ability to acquire new knowledge through instruction or experience) and memory (the process by which knowledge is retained over time) are both closely linked examples of neural plasticity.

Songbirds learn to sing by imitation, much the same way that humans learn language. Studies of songbirds have demonstrated that neural circuits involved in song recognition and song production undergo distinct changes that relate to song development. **Functional brain imaging** studies of string instrument players have shown that cortical representation of the fingers of their left hands increases in proportion to the length of time they practiced as children, during a period of 5 to 20 years. Similar studies have suggested that regions of the cortex that are unable to be activated by visual stimulation in people blind from birth become functionally linked to touch stimulation of the fingers associated with **Braille** reading.

The underlying mechanisms for learning and memory are currently not very well understood. Scientists believe that the answers lie at the synapse, and that activity-dependent changes in synapses play an important role in learning and memory. The idea of activity-dependent plasticity of synapses was proposed more than 50 years ago by Donald Hebb, described by many as the father of neuropsychology. He suggested that synapses between cells that are actively communicating with each other are maintained, whereas those that are not in active use are reduced or eliminated. The exact relationship between activity-dependent synaptic plasticity and learning and memory is one of the most intensely studied areas in neuroscience today.

Two cellular phenomena, namely **long-term potentiation** and **long-term depression**, have been proposed as potential candidates for explaining the molecular basis of learning and memory. Long-term potentiation is the long-lasting strengthening of a synapse between two neurons. It depends on the activation of the N-methyl-D-aspartate (NMDA) receptor present on the postsynaptic neuron by the neurotransmitter **glutamate** released from the presynaptic neuron, and the flow of calcium ions into the postsynaptic neuron. Drugs that block the NMDA receptor disrupt learning in rats. Targeted deletion of NMDA receptors in mice prevents long-term potentiation in the hippocampus and impairs their ability to learn **spatial** cues (information pertaining to the location of objects).

Conversely, increased activity of the NMDA receptor has been shown to produce increased long-term potentiation. In turn, this creates "smart mice" capable of improved spatial learning. Long-term depression is a process similar to long-term potentiation, but it involves weakening of the synapse instead. Long-term depression in the cerebellum is thought to be important for learning motor skills, and in the hippocampus for clearing traces of old memories. Scientists are still a long way from understanding the complex behavior of learning and memory in humans since plasticity associated with some seemingly simple reflexes, such as the sudden withdrawal of a hand in response to a pain stimulus, is also poorly understood at this time.

NEURAL PLASTICITY AFTER INJURY

Neural plasticity also forms the basis for the ability to recover from brain damage caused by injury or disease. Brain damage can impair any of the number of actions that we take for granted. When damage occurs, the brain attempts to compensate for loss in several different ways. It might form new connections between spared neurons, reroute circuits to different regions of the brain, sprout new axonal branches, make behavioral adjustments, or even attempt to re-grow severed axons.

Throughout history, striking examples of functional recovery after brain damage have been documented. In some cases, stroke patients who have lost the ability to speak or to use a hand have been shown to regain some or most of their lost function within weeks or months of therapy. Functional imaging techniques, such as positron emission tomography and functional magnetic resonance imaging, enable scientists to look inside the brain of recovering patients while they perform a certain task. These techniques have greatly contributed to our understanding of how the brain reorganizes its circuits in response to damage. Some recovered stroke patients, for example, use an alternate pathway of nerve fibers to control their affected hand, instead of the usual **corticospinal tract**—the bundle of nerve fibers that travels from the cortex and excites motor neurons of the spinal cord to cause muscular contractions of the hand. Some recovered stroke patients engage unusual parts of their motor cortex, and sometimes even their visual cortex, to move the fingers of their stroke-affected hand. Similar studies on children with epilepsy have shown their ability to recover lost function even after drastic surgeries involving removal of an entire hemisphere of the cerebrum, and studies of people blind from birth have shown rerouting of neural circuits to parts of the visual cortex to perform tasks of tactile discrimination such as reading Braille.

Unfortunately, the attempts made by the brain to compensate for damage are not always successful or even sufficient to promote recovery of lost function. When this happens, permanent disability can result. The extent of disability can range from cognitive impairment, sensory loss, and movement problems to a persistent vegetative state, coma, and death. For example, in people with multiple sclerosis, the work of a faulty immune system results in damage to myelin, axonal degeneration, and a wide range of movement and sensory disorders due to the inability of injured axons to properly transmit nerve impulses. Attempts to compensate for myelin loss include remyelination by oligodendrocytes, as well as redistribution of sodium channels to the bare internodes. However, these attempts often become less effective as the disease progresses. In injuries such as traumatic brain injury and spinal cord injury, attempts made by severed central nervous system axons to regenerate are thwarted by molecules unique to the central nervous system.

In people with Huntington's disease, an inherited gene mutation results in the death of neurons in the basal ganglia and cerebral cortex and a variety of physical, cognitive, and psychiatric disorders. Loss of **dopamine**-secreting neurons in people with Parkinson's disease impairs muscular control so that movement, speech, and posture are affected. In people with Alzheimer's disease, death of neurons in regions of the brain such as the hippocampus and the cerebral cortex result in the gradual loss of a variety of mental functions, including memory or the ability to carry out even the simplest of tasks (Figure 7.3). Although studies have revealed that the adult brain continues to generate new neurons in select regions, it is not clear why such neurons are unable to replace lost cells in some diseases. There is currently no way of fixing highly specialized neural circuits in the damaged brain, or accurately determining whether a lost function can be recovered. Scientists continue to investigate neural plasticity, the exact conditions that permit repair and recovery of function following brain damage, and the possibility of harnessing the potential of stem cells in the repair process.

KEY POINTS

Nature as well as nurture influence brain development in important ways. Experience is essential for continued development of neural circuits after birth. Neural plasticity is the

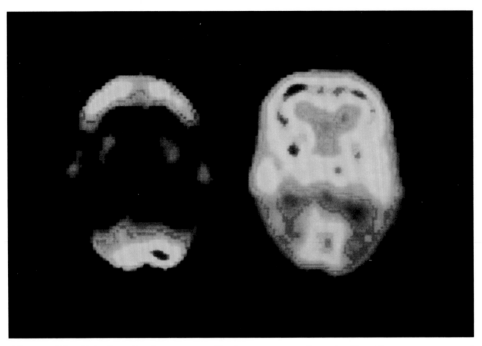

Figure 7.3 Alzheimer's disease results from neuron loss in the hippocampus and cerebral cortex. Shown here are positron emission tomography (PET) scans of a healthy human brain (right) as compared to one afflicted with Alzheimer's.

ability of the brain to reorganize its neural circuits in response to experience. It is exemplified every day in life, from birth to maturity, as we learn a new skill, memorize an experience, adapt to a loss, or recover from injury. The basic mechanisms that support neural plasticity include the formation and elimination of synapses, persistence of neurogenesis in some parts of the brain, activity-dependent fine-tuning of neural connections, rewiring of neural circuits, and death of neurons.

■ **Learn more about the contents of this chapter**   Search the Internet for *learning and memory*, *dopamine*, and *Torsten Wiesel*.

8 | Advances in Neuroscience

The past 100 years have witnessed an explosion of scientific knowledge in neuroscience. This has been brought about, in large part, due to progress in other areas of science such as medicine, physics, chemistry, mathematics, and biology. The design of powerful microscopes made it possible to examine the nervous system at the molecular scale. The understanding of biochemical events that affect nervous system function led to the large-scale production of medicinal drugs that maintain health and treat mental illnesses. The decoding of the human genome, that is, the chemical letters that make us who we are, is bringing us closer to understanding brain diseases. The discovery of fundamental biological processes that control gene expression is setting the stage for the development of a new generation of treatments and potential cures for a variety of neurological disorders. The growth of scientific knowledge has been, and continues to be, remarkable. This chapter provides a glimpse into some of the most influential discoveries in neuroscience.

LAYING THE FOUNDATION

During the turn of the twentieth century, it was widely believed that the nervous system was made up of a meshwork of nerve fibers that connected to one another like blood vessels within the circulatory system. This "reticular" notion of the nervous system was challenged by Spanish histologist Santiago Ramón y Cajal, whose research strongly supported the "neuron doctrine," which states that the basic unit of the nervous system is the neuron, and that the nervous system is made up of individual neurons that are adjacent, but not physically continuous with each other.

Cajal's findings were made possible by a then state-of-the-art tissue staining technique developed by Italian researcher Camillo Golgi. Unlike earlier methods, the Golgi staining technique allowed researchers to view details of the entire neuron, i.e., cell body, dendrites, and axon. Armed with the Golgi stain and a microscope, Cajal immersed himself in the study of the fine structure of the nervous system. In those days, methods to photograph microscopic structures were not well developed. Therefore Cajal documented his scientific observations by means of detailed drawings (Figure 8.1). The remarkable accuracy of his drawings of individual neurons and neural circuitry within the brain and spinal cord became appreciated only years later when modern tools of cellular imaging became available. Cajal's work, among other things, led to the conclusion that a neuron is indeed the basic unit of the nervous system, a conclusion that forms the basic principle of the organization of the nervous system. In 1906, the Nobel Prize for Physiology or Medicine was awarded to Cajal for his marvelous illumination of the cellular architecture of the nervous system. The prize was also awarded to Camillo Golgi for his discovery of the technique that made such an illumination possible.

Another major milestone in our understanding of the nervous system came during the 1950s from the work of two English physiologists, Alan Lloyd Hodgkin and Andrew Fielding Huxley. Hodgkin and Huxley focused their work on determining the mechanisms that control the way neurons conduct impulses. For their experiments, they chose the giant squid whose unusually

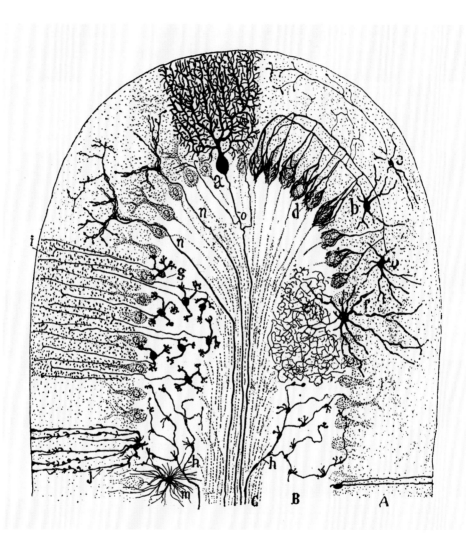

Figure 8.1 In the late nineteenth century, a staining technique invented by Italian researcher Camillo Golgi allowed scientists to perform microscopic study of the nervous system. Using this method, Spanish physician Santiago Ramón y Cajal created this detailed drawing of nerve cells.

large axons allowed ease of manipulation and experimentation with the only tools available in those days. They placed the squid axon in a bath of seawater, inserted an electronic device into the axon, and applied a voltage stimulus to it. They studied the action potential that was produced in response to the stimulus by measuring the **membrane potential** as the impulse traveled along the axon. They performed their studies under various conditions, clamping the cell at a specific voltage and varying the concentration of ions within the axon.

From their analyses, Hodgkin and Huxley were able to determine that the electrical activity of the axonal cell membrane is influenced by the flow of ions across the membrane. They developed a mathematical model, widely known as the Hodgkin and Huxley model, which gave scientists a basic understanding of how action potentials travel along axons. This was at a time when there was no detailed knowledge about the molecular composition of the axon membrane. Hodgkin and Huxley's findings led them to hypothesize the existence of **ion channels** along the axon membrane, which would be discovered only decades later. For their lasting contribution to the understanding of how neurons conduct impulses, Hodgkin and Huxley were jointly awarded the Nobel Prize in Physiology or Medicine in 1963.

The invention of **electron microscopy** in the 1950s and 1960s allowed scientists to examine the nervous system in greater detail. Their findings revealed the exquisite complexity of the neuron and confirmed the presence of synapses as suggested by Cajal. Meanwhile, scientists had already begun to discover neurotransmitters as chemicals that allow the transmission of signals across the synapse. Acetylcholine was the first neurotransmitter to be discovered. Acetylcholine functions at many regions throughout the nervous system. It is the neurotransmitter that is responsible for stimulation of muscles. It is also the neurotransmitter that is in short supply in people with Alzheimer's disease. German biologist Otto Loewi discovered this neurotransmitter and won the Nobel Prize for his work. Before long, many other neurotransmitters began to be discovered, including norepinephrine, the neurotransmitter associated with bringing the nervous system into high alert; GABA, an inhibitory neurotransmitter that acts like a brake to the excitatory neurotransmitters that lead to anxiety; glutamate, the most common neurotransmitter in the central nervous system; and serotonin, the neurotransmitter that is closely associated with emotion and mood. With an increased understanding of the role of neurotransmitters in brain function, it became clear that human behavior is a biochemical event that can be altered by specially formulated drugs. Drug treatments became available for previously untreatable diseases such as Parkinson's disease, schizophrenia, and epilepsy.

The discovery of neurotrophic factors transformed our understanding of mechanisms that regulate brain development. Neurotrophic factors are potent signaling molecules that nourish neurons, ensuring their growth, differentiation, and survival. The first neurotrophic factor to be discovered was nerve growth factor, or NGF. It was identified in the 1950s by Italian developmental biologist Rita Levi-Montalcini as a chemical that induced growth and differentiation of developing chicken neurons. The discovery of NGF, and the formulation of the neurotrophic factor hypothesis (which states that neurons are dependent on neurotrophic factors supplied by their target tissue for survival, growth, and differentiation) have been crucial in driving efforts toward the discovery of several other neurotrophic factors. Due to the crucial role that they play in the development and maintenance of the nervous system, and because of their potential use in the treatment of neurological diseases, neurotrophic factors continue to be investigated today with great intensity. For her discovery of the fundamental role of NGF in the development and functioning of the nervous system, Levi-Montalcini was awarded the Nobel Prize in Physiology or Medicine in 1986.

THE NEW MILLENNIUM

At the dawn of the twenty-first century, neuroscience research continues to march forward. There are more neuroscientists than ever before. Much of neuroscience research today is focused on unraveling the intricate mechanisms that direct neurons to stay alive, multiply in number, become specialized, perform assigned tasks, and die. Many major genes, proteins, and signaling pathways that are involved in nervous system function are being identified for the first time. This is bringing us closer to a better understanding of some of the most devastating **neurodegenerative disorders** that plague our time.

Neurodegenerative disorders, characterized by the progressive disintegration of the nervous system, are caused by the death or malfunctioning of neurons. Scientists now know that the cause for Huntington's disease is a defective gene that kills neurons in the brain and robs individuals of their mental and physical capabilities. Scientists also know the protein that the Huntington gene encodes, but exactly how the protein cripples the brain remains a mystery. It continues to be actively investigated.

Major research advances have also been made in the area of Parkinson's disease, which is caused by a decrease in the neurotransmitter dopamine. This is due to the death of dopamine-producing neurons in a region of the brain that controls movement. While discoveries of the past have led to successful treatments that replace the lost dopamine, current efforts in Parkinson's disease are focused on understanding trigger factors, underlying molecular mechanisms, and ways to cure the disease. Because of such efforts, the possibility of halting disease progression, restoring lost function, and preventing Parkinson's disease altogether is closer to being materialized than ever before. Similar efforts are also being made toward treatments for and a better understanding of the complex biology behind other neurodegenerative diseases such as Alzheimer's disease and multiple sclerosis.

Figure 8.2 Imaging technology allows researchers to observe processes and brain function without invasive surgery. At left, a patient enters a functional magnetic resonance imaging machine (fMRI) that will monitor brain activity over a period of seconds to minutes. At right, a scientist views images created by an fMRI machine.

Scientists today are studying the inner workings of the living brain using powerful, safe, and noninvasive methods of **neuroimaging** (Figure 8.2). They are able to study changes in brain metabolism, obtain high-resolution images of the brain, and measure functional changes in brain activity in real time. This is allowing the unprecedented study of the living brain at various stages during development, both in health and disease.

Recently, a decade-long study of normal brain development from ages 4 to 21 revealed the timing of the maturation of various centers in the brain. It showed, for example, that the first areas of the brain to mature are those that perform basic tasks such as processing information related to the senses and movement. "Higher-order" brain centers, such as those for reasoning and problem solving, were the last to mature.

Neuroimaging studies are beginning to shed light on neurodevelopmental disorders such as attention-deficit hyperactivity disorder (ADHD), dyslexia, and autism, which continue to baffle scientists. Imaging scans have revealed that in people with dyslexia (a disorder that causes reading difficulties), normal patterns of activation in regions of the brain involved in reading are disrupted. This revelation led scientists to devise an intervention program for children with dyslexia. The program not only led to improved reading ability, but also helped permanently rewire the brain in a way that more closely resembled patterns of activation displayed in the brain of typical readers. Other imaging studies have also identified patterns of brain activity that are unique to individuals with ADHD. Information obtained from these types of studies is now allowing scientists to produce in-depth regional maps of the brain, better understand the biological basis for developmental disorders of the brain, and identify strategies for accurate diagnosis and effective treatment.

Challenging previously held beliefs, scientists are searching for ways to fix broken circuits in debilitating central nervous system injuries and diseases such as spinal cord injury, traumatic brain injury, and multiple sclerosis—once thought impossible to treat. They are investigating strategies to modify the central nervous system environment so that it becomes hospitable for regrowth of severed axons. Scientists have already identified some of the hurdles that severed axons face within the central nervous system as they struggle to recover. Transplanting stem cells and other specialized cells, scientists are demonstrating that it is possible to restore myelin around damaged axons and improve movement in experimental models of nervous system injury. They are developing strategies to provide structural support for the regrowth of axons, and to deliver nourishing, growth-promoting neurotrophic factors. They are studying ways to boost the body's own repair mechanisms within the injured nervous system. Scientists are also engineering new brain-machine programs that would enable severely paralyzed individuals to control their movements with special electronic devices, using the power of their thought alone. Nerve disease or injury often results in neuropathic pain, which is a burning, searing type of pain that can profoundly affect the quality of life in affected individuals. Scientists are studying the underlying molecular mechanisms of pain perception with the goal of finding better treatments.

FROM DISCOVERIES TO CURES

Scientists hope that they may someday be able to replace neurons that have been lost to disease or injury by harnessing the power of stem cell technology. They hope to be able to swap an abnormal, disease-causing gene with a normal copy through gene therapy, and to selectively suppress the activity of misbehaving genes through gene silencing. Suppressing wayward genes has already been used to successfully treat Huntington's disease in experiments on mice. The 2006 Nobel Prize for Physiology or Medicine was awarded to American scientists Andrew Fire and Craig Mello for their discovery of of RNA interference, or RNAi, a powerful mechanism that forms the basis for gene silencing. It is only a matter of time before such discoveries are translated into cures for people with neurological disorders.

■ **Learn more about the contents of this chapter** Search the Internet for *Alan Lloyd Hodgkin, magnetic resonance imaging,* and *computed tomography.*

Glossary

Acetylcholine A type of neurotransmitter.

Action potential The explosion in electrical activity created by traveling nerve impulses.

Axon An extension of a neuron that carries information away from the cell body.

Basal ganglia A group of structures in the brain associated with movement, cognition, emotion, and learning.

Blastocyst The ball of the rapidly expanding embryonic cell cluster.

Body-axis The imaginary longitudinal line around which the body develops.

Bone morphogenetic protein The group of growth factors known to control the body plan of the developing embryo.

Braille A reading and writing system for the blind, composed of raised dots in place of letters.

Brain stem The region of the brain that connects the brain with the spinal cord.

Cell adhesion molecule A molecule that allows cells to stick to other cells or surrounding noncellular structures.

Cell body Portion of the cell in which the nucleus is located.

Cell fate specification Molecular mechanism by which a cell is instructed take on a certain morphology and function.

Cell transplantation The transfer of cells from one place or position to another.

Central nervous system The part of the nervous system that is composed of the brain and spinal cord.

Cerebellum The region of the brain that controls balance and coordination.

Cerebral cortex The outermost layer of the brain.

Cerebrospinal fluid Fluid that supports the brain and acts as a shock absorber during rapid head movements.

Cerebrum The region of the brain that controls conscious thought and voluntary movement.

Cholesterol A type of fat that is present in cell membranes of all cells.

Corticospinal tract The bundle of nerve fibers that travels from the motor cortex to excite motor neurons of the spinal cord to cause muscular contractions of the hand.

Crossed representation Left-right reversal in the central nervous system.

Cytoskeletal protein The protein that makes up the cellular "scaffolding" or "skeleton" within the cell; proteins that make up the structural elements of a cell.

Dendrite The extension of neurons that brings information to the cell body.

Depolarization Decrease in the polarity of the electrically charged membrane.

Differentiation The process by which cells mature and prepare to take on specific jobs.

Dopamine The neurotransmitter that is associated with movement and emotion.

Dorsal Pertaining to the back of the body.

Dorsal blastopore lip The margin or lip of the blastula wall that is necessary for the development of neural tissue.

Ectoderm Embryonic tissue that gives rise to the nervous system.

Electrochemical process The neuronal process that involves conversion of chemical signals to electrical signals.

Electron microscopy Type of microscope that uses electrons to create an image of the target; it can magnify an object up to two million times its original size.

Embryonic stem cell A cell that has the potential to give rise to every cell type of an individual.

Endocrine system The system of glands that secrete hormones.

Endoderm The embryonic tissue that gives rise to the pharynx, esophagus, stomach, intestines, and associated glands.

Extracellular Describes an object that is located or an action that takes place outside of a cell.

Extracellular matrix The noncellular environment that surrounds cells within a tissue.

Fight-or-flight response The body's instinctive response to perceived threat or danger.

Filopodia Fingerlike projections of a growth cone.

Forebrain The largest part of the brain; controls cognition, sensation, and movement; regulates temperature, reproductive functions, eating, sleeping, and display of emotions.

Functional brain imaging An imaging technique that enables visualization of information processing by specific regions of the brain.

Gene expression The process by which a cell's gene sequence is "expressed" to achieve a certain function.

Gene therapy The insertion of genes into an individual's cells and tissues to treat disease.

Glia The basic cellular units that support the nervous system.

Glutamate The most common neurotransmitter in the central nervous system.

Glycolipids A type of fat that is present in cell membranes of all cells.

Gray matter The portion of the brain mostly composed of cell bodies of neurons.

Growth cone The advancing tip of an axon.

Growth factor The naturally occurring protein capable of stimulating cell proliferation and cell differentiation.

Guidance molecule The molecule that guides advancing axons to their synaptic targets.

Gyri Ridges in the surface of the cerebral cortex.

Hindbrain The region of the brain that coordinates movement, posture, equilibrium, and sleep patterns; regulates autonomous but essential functions, such as breathing and blood circulation.

Homeobox DNA sequence found within genes involved in the regulation of development.

Huntington's disease The genetic disorder that leads to death of neurons in the basal ganglia and cerebral cortex.

Hypothalamus The region of the brain that regulates metabolic and autonomic functions.

Implantation The physical anchoring of the blastocyst to the womb.

Interneuron A neuron that sends information between sensory neurons and motor neurons.

Internode A myelinated region between the nodes of Ranvier.

Ion channel The pore-like protein that controls the flow of ions in and out of a cell.

Jagged The ligand or activator of the Notch receptor protein.

Kallman syndrome A disorder in which neurons that produce sex hormones and neurons that sense odors fail to migrate to their proper locations.

Lissencephaly The gene-linked brain malformation characterized by a smooth cerebral cortex as a result of defective neuronal migration.

Long-term depression The weakening of a synapse that lasts from hours to days.

Long-term potentiation Long-lasting strengthening of a synapse between two neurons.

Membrane potential The electrical potential difference (voltage) across a cell's plasma membrane.

Meninges Layers of tissue that cover the brain and lie just beneath the skull.

Mesoderm Embryonic tissue that gives rise to heart, bone marrow, blood, bones, muscles and reproductive organs.

Midbrain The small region of the brain that is located between the forebrain and the hindbrain; forms a major part of the brain stem.

Motor cortex The regions of the cerebral cortex involved in the planning, control, and execution of voluntary motor function.

Multiple sclerosis A disease that results when myelin is under attack by the person's own immune system.

Myelin The insulation that surrounds some types of axons.

Myelin basic protein An important component of myelin membrane.

Neural crest Cells that give rise to the peripheral nervous system.

Neural plasticity Changes that occur within the nervous system.

Neural plate The upper plate of ectoderm that differentiates into the neural tube and neural crest.

Neural tube Part of the developing vertebrate embryo that gives rise to the central nervous system.

Neurodegenerative disorders Diseases and disorders caused by the progressive disintegration of the nervous system.

Neurogenesis The production of neurons.

Neuroimaging Technique to either directly or indirectly visualize the structure and function of the brain.

Neuromuscular junction The synapse between a motor neuron and a muscle cell.

Neuron A nerve cell; a basic cellular unit that relays messages between the brain and the rest of the body.

Neurotransmitter A chemical released into a synapse by the transmitting neuron.

Neurotrophic factors Molecules that are required for growth and survival of developing neurons, and maintenance of adult neurons.

N-methyl-D-aspartate (NMDA) A synthetic chemical that mimics the action of the neurotransmitter glutamate.

Nodal An important regulator of early body axis formation.

Nodes of Ranvier Bare regions of axons that are not myelinated.

Notch A key regulator in the process of cell specification.

Ocular dominance The preference of neurons for stimulation from one eye or the other.

Oligodendrocyte A specialized glial cell that myelinates axons of the central nervous system.

Oligodendrocyte precursors Developing cells that will form the oligodendrocytes.

Parkinson's disease A disorder of the brain characterized by shaking and difficulty with walking and movement.

Pelizaeus-Merzbacher disease A neurological condition in which coordination, motor abilities, and intellectual function gradually deteriorate.

Peripheral nervous system The part of the nervous system outside the brain and spinal cord.

Phospholipid A type of fat that is a major part of all biological membranes.

Pituitary gland The pea-sized gland situated at the base of the brain that secretes hormones.

Polarized A state of opposition as in, for example, the difference in electrical charge between the inside and outside of a neuron.

Postsynaptic cell The cell whose behavior is influenced by the presynaptic neuron.

Presynaptic Referring neuron that directly influences the post-synaptic cell.

Primary visual cortex The area of the cortex that is involved in processing of visual stimuli.

Primitive streak The narrow line of cells that precedes the formation of the three germ layers in the embryo.

Proteolipid protein One of the protein components of the myelin membrane.

Radial glia Elongated glial cells that provide tracks for these neurons to migrate.

Saltatory conduction A type of conduction in which action potentials leap from one node of Ranvier to the next.

Schwann cell A specialized glial cell that myelinates axons of the peripheral nervous system.

Sensory cortex The part of the brain that receives messages from the sense organs.

Somatosensory cortex The part of the sensory cortex that responds to touch.

Sonic hedgehog The positional signal that controls cell differentiation.

Spatial Pertaining to space or location.

Stroke A rupture or blockage of a blood vessel in the brain.

Subventricular zone The region immediately adjacent to the ventricular zone.

Sulci Depressions or fissures in the surface of the brain.

Synapse A small gap through which information flows from one neuron to another cell.

Synaptic cleft A narrow region that separates the pre- and postsynaptic cells.

Thalamocortical axons Fibers that connect the thalamus to the cortex.

Thalamus The part of the brain that performs many functions, including relay of signals to the cerebral cortex.

Touch circuits A network of neurons that makes the sensation of touch possible.

Tourette syndrome A condition of the nervous system characterized by involuntary movements and vocalizations known as tics.

Transcription factor The protein that regulates gene expression.

Ventral Pertaining to the underside of an animal's body, or the front of the human body.

Ventricular zone A region of active cell division where neurons are produced.

Visual circuitry The neural network that makes vision possible.

Voltage The force or strength of electricity in a circuit.

White matter The portion of the brain or spinal cord that mostly contains myelinated axons.

Bibliography

Arroyo, E.J., and S.S. Scherer. "On the Molecular Architecture of Myelinated Fibers." *Histochemistry and Cell Biology* 113 (2000): 1–18.

Baumann, N., and D. Pham-Dinh. "Biology of Oligodendrocyte and Myelin in the Mammalian Central Nervous System." *Physiological Reviews* 81 (2001): 871–927.

Ben-Arie N., H.J. Bellen, D.L. Armstrong, A.E. McCall, P.R. Gordadze, Q. Guo, M.M. Matzuk, and H.Y. Zoghbi. "Math1 Is Essential for Generation of Cerebellar Granule Neurons." *Nature* 390 (1997): 169–72.

Black, J.A., J.D. Kocsis, and S.G. Waxman. "Ion Channel Organization of the Myelinated Fiber." *Trends Neuroscience* 13 (1990): 48–54.

Briscoe, J., and J. Ericson. "The Specification of Neuronal Identity by Graded Sonic Hedgehog Signaling." *Seminars in Cell and Developmental Biology* 10 (1999): 353–362.

Chao, M.V., R. Rajagopal, and F.S. Lee. "Neurotrophin Signalling in Health and Disease." *Clinical Science* 110 (2006): 167–173.

Dontchev, V.D., and P.C. Letourneau. "Growth Cones Integrate Signaling From Multiple Guidance Cues." *Journal of Histochemistry and Cytochemistry* 51 (2003): 435–444.

Evans P.D., J.R. Anders, E.J. Vallender, S.S. Choi , and B.T. Lahn. "Reconstructing the Evolutionary History of Microcephalin, a Gene Controlling Human Brain Size." *Human Molecular Genetics* 13 (2004): 1139–1145.

Evans P.D., J.R. Anderson, E.J. Vallender, S.L. Gilbert, C.M. Malcom, S. Dorus, and B.T. Lahn. "Adaptive Evolution of ASPM, a Major Determinant of Cerebral Cortical Size in Humans." *Human Molecular Genetics* 13 (2004): 489–494.

Gilbert, Scott F. *Developmental Biology.* 6th ed. Sunderland, Mass.: Sinauer Associates, 2000.

Glass, D.J., and G.D. Yancopoulos. "Sequential Roles of Agrin, MuSK and Rapsyn During Neuromuscular Junction Formation." *Current Opinions in Neurobiology* 7 (1997): 379–384.

Goodman, C.S., M.J. Bastiani, C.Q. Doe, et al. "Cell Recognition During Neuronal Development." *Science* 225 (1984): 1271–1279.

Gross, C.G. "Neurogenesis in the Adult Brain: Death of a Dogma." *Nature Review Neuroscience* 1 (2000): 67–73.

Hemmati-Brivanlou, A., and D. Melton. "Vertebrate Embryonic Cells Will Become Nerve Cells Unless Told Otherwise." *Cell* 88 (1997): 13–17.

Huttenlocher, Peter R. *Neural Plasticity: The Effects of Environment on the Development of the Cerebral Cortex.* Cambridge, Mass.: Harvard University Press, 2002.

Kakizawa, S., M. Yamasaki., M. Watanabe, and M. Kano. "Critical Period for Activity-dependent Synapse Elimination in Developing Cerebellum. *Journal of Neuroscience* 20 (2000): 4954–4961.

Kandel, Eric R., James H. Schwartz, and Thomas M. Jessell, eds. *Principles of Neural Science.* 4th ed. New York: McGraw-Hill, 2000.

Kringelbach, M., and A. Engell. "Development and Plasticity in the Brain." *Psyke & Logos* 18 (1997): 266–286.

Lemke, G. "Glial Control of Neuronal Development." *Annual Reviews in Neuroscience* 24 (2001): 87–105.

Lois, C., and A. Alvarez-Buylla. "Long-distance Neuronal Migration in the Adult Mammalian Brain." *Science* 264 (1994): 1145–1148.

Louvi, A., and S. Artavanis-Tsakonas. "Notch Signalling in Vertebrate Neural Development." *Nature Reviews Neuroscience* 7 (2006): 93–102.

Majewska, A.K., and M. Sur. "Plasticity and Specificity of Cortical Processing Networks." *Trends in Neuroscience* 29 (2006): 323–329.

McAllister, A.K. "Conserved Cues for Axon and Dendrite Growth in the Developing Cortex." *Neuron* 33 (2002): 2–4.

McHugh, T.J., I.K. Blum, J.Z. Tsien, S. Tonegawa, M.A. Wilson. "Impaired Hippocampal Representation of Space in CA1-specific NMDAR1 Knockout Mice." *Cell* 87 (1996): 1339–1349.

Morris, R.G., E. Anderson, G.S. Lynch, and M. Baudry. "Selective Impairment of Learning and Blockade of Long-term Potentiation by an N-methyl-D-aspartate Receptor Antagonist, AP5." *Nature* 319 (1986): 774–776.

Rakic, P. "A Small Step for the Cell, a Giant Leap for Mankind: A Hypothesis of Neocortical Expansion During Evolution." *Trends in Neuroscience* 18 (1995): 383–388.

Roth, G., and U. Dicke. "Evolution of the Brain and Intelligence." *Trends in Cognitive Sciences* 9 (2005): 250–257.

Schier, A.F., and M.M. Shen. "Nodal Signalling in Vertebrate Development." *Nature* 403 (2000): 385–389.

Sherman, D.L., and P. Brophy. "Mechanisms of Axon Ensheathment and Myelin Growth." *Nature Reviews Neuroscience* 6 (2005): 683–690.

Shi, S.H., D.N. Cox , D. Wang, L.Y. Jan , and Y.N. Jan. "Control of Dendrite Arborization by an Ig Family Member, Dendrite Arborization and Synapse Maturation 1 (Dasm1)." *Proceedings of the National Academy of Sciences USA* 101 (2004): 13341–13345.

Tang, B.L. "Molecular Determinants of Human Brain Size." *Biochemical and Biophysical Research Communications* 345 (2006): 911–916.

Waxman, Stephen G. *Correlative Neuroanatomy*. Stamford, Conn.: Appleton and Lange, 1996.

Waxman, S.G., and J.A. Black. "Unmyelinated and Myelinated Axon Membrane From Rat Corpus Callosum: Differences in Macromolecular Structure." *Brain Research* 453 (1988): 337–343.

Wen, Z., and J.Q. Zheng. "Directional Guidance of Nerve Growth Cones." *Current Opinions in Neurobiology* 16 (2006): 52–58.

Wieloch T., and K. Nikolich. "Mechanisms of Neural Plasticity Following Brain Injury." *Current Opinions in Neurobiology* 16 (2006): 258–264.

Further Reading

Coen, Enrico. *The Art of Genes: How Organisms Make Themselves.* New York: Oxford University Press, 2000.

Drubach, Daniel. *The Brain Explained.* Upper Saddle River, N.J.: Prentice Hall, 2000.

Dubin, Mark, and Lauren M. Sompayrac. *How the Brain Works.* Malden, Mass.: Blackwell Publishing, 2002.

Finger, Stanley. *Origins of Neuroscience: A History of Explorations into Brain Function.* New York: Oxford University Press, 2001.

Kandel, Eric R. *In Search of Memory: The Emergence of a New Science of Mind.* New York: W. W. Norton, 2006.

Levi-Montalcini, R., and P. Calissano. "The Nerve-growth Factor." *Scientific American* 240 (1979): 44–53.

McCrone, John. *The Ape That Spoke: Language and the Evolution of the Human Mind.* New York: William Morrow and Company, 1991.

Nolte, John. *The Human Brain: An Introduction to Its Functional Anatomy.* 5th ed. St. Louis, Mo.: C.V. Mosby, 2002.

Nusslein-Volhard, Christiane. *Coming to Life: How Genes Drive Development.* San Diego, Calif.: Kales, 2006.

Olsen, S. "The Synapse Revealed." *Howard Hughes Medical Institute Bulletin* 17 (2004): 14–23.

Ramón Cajal, Santiago. *Advice for a Young Investigator.* New ed. Cambridge, Mass.: The MIT Press, 2004.

———. *Recollections of My Life.* Reprint, Cambridge, Mass.: The MIT Press, 1989.

Rapport, Richard. *Nerve Endings: The Discovery of the Synapse.* New York: W.W. Norton, 2005.

Ridley, Matt. *Nature via Nurture: Genes, Experience, and What Makes Us Human.* New York: HarperCollins, 2003.

Rowan, Pete. *Big Head! A Book about Your Brain and Your Head.* New York: Alfred A. Knopf, 1998.

Schatz, C.J. "The Developing Brain." *Scientific American* 267 (1992): 60–67.

Upledger, John E. *A Brain Is Born: Exploring the Birth and Development of the Central Nervous System*, Berkeley, Calif.: North Atlantic Books, 1997.

Web Sites

Brain Basics: Know Your Brain
http://www.ninds.nih.gov/disorders/brain_basics/know_your_brain .htm#art

Brain Briefings
http://www.sfn.org/briefings

Encyclopedia of Life Sciences
http://www.els.net

HHMI Bulletin
http://www.hhmi.org

Neuroscience for Kids
http://faculty.washington.edu/chudler/introb.html

News from the Neurosciences: Embryological Development of the Human Brain
http://www.newhorizons.org/index.html

A Science Odyssey: In Search of Ourselves
http://www.pbs.org/wgbh/aso/thenandnow/humbeh.html

Picture Credits

2: © Infobase Publishing
3: © Infobase Publishing
5: © Infobase Publishing
7: © Infobase Publishing
12: © Infobase Publishing
15: © Infobase Publishing
17: © Infobase Publishing
19: © Infobase Publishing
26: © Infobase Publishing
28: © Infobase Publishing
33: © Infobase Publishing
38: © DR TORSTEN WITTMANN/
 Photo Researchers, Inc.
42: © Infobase Publishing
43: © Infobase Publishing

47: © Infobase Publishing
48: © Dr. Don W. Fawcett/Visuals
 Unlimited
54: © Steve Gschmeissner/
 Photo Researchers, Inc.
57: © Infobase Publishing
64: © Dr. John Zajicek/Photo
 Researchers, Inc.
67: © Infobase Publishing
69: © Infobase Publishing
74: © Science Source
77: © The Granger Collection,
 New York
81: © Mark Harmel/Photo
 Researchers, Inc.

Index

About the Author

Lakshmi Bangalore, Ph.D., is a scientific liaison officer at the Center for Neuroscience and Regeneration Research and a faculty member in the Department of Neurology at Yale University School of Medicine. She works at the interface between science and society and supports a variety of activities related to research communication and information dissemination. Dr. Bangalore obtained her doctoral degree in molecular, cellular, and developmental biology from Yale University, and her bachelor's degree in chemistry, botany, and zoology from MES College in Bangalore, India. Her research has focused on mechanisms of signal transduction from outside a cell to inside, and on processes that regulate cell growth, proliferation, and differentiation. Dr. Bangalore enjoys writing about discoveries in neuroscience for the general public and lives in Madison, Connecticut, with her husband and two daughters.

About the Editor

Eric H. Chudler, Ph.D., is a research neuroscientist who has investigated the brain mechanisms of pain and nociception since 1978. He is currently a research associate professor in the University of Washington Department of Bioengineering and director of education and outreach at University of Washington Engineered Biomaterials. Dr. Chudler's research interests focus on how areas of the central nervous system (cerebral cortex and basal ganglia) process information related to pain.